THE BISCOFF

COOKIE & SPREAD

COOKBOOK

THE BISCOFF COOKIE & SPREAD

COOKBOOK

Irresistible Cupcakes, Cookies,
Confections, and More

KATRINA BAHL

The Countryman Press
Woodstock, VT
www.countrymanpress.com

Every effort has been made to ensure that the information contained in this book is complete and accurate. The publisher is not responsible for your specific health or allergy needs that may require medical supervision.

Biscoff Cookies and Biscoff Spread do not contain any nuts and are 100% nut free. They are both produced in a facility that never uses shared equipment for other products containing nuts.

• • • • • • ● • ● • • • • • •

Text and photographs © 2014 by Katrina Bahl

Cover and interior design by Nancy Freeborn

Published by The Countryman Press
P.O. Box 748, Woodstock, VT 05091

Distributed by W. W. Norton & Company, Inc.
500 Fifth Avenue, New York, NY 10110

The Biscoff Cookie & Spread Book
ISBN: 978-1-58157-226-1

Printed in the United States
10 9 8 7 6 5 4 3 2 1

To Chuck, my best friend.
I am a better person because of you.

———•———

To Luke and Tim, my joys.
I love being your mom.

CONTENTS

FOREWORD

Two brothers making traditional cookies at their Belgian bakery in the 1930s; a mom in Belgium with a creative idea for a reality TV show; and a young boy in Ohio struggling to enjoy his family's holiday traditions despite a peanut allergy. Who would have thought that these three stories would intersect? But intersect they did, and the happy result is this cookbook.

We begin in the Belgian town of Lembeke, the home of the Boone brothers, both bakers. Like most Belgians, the brothers were especially fond of a traditional Belgian cookie known as speculoos (today called Biscoff). These cookies' flavor and texture are unique, owing to a magical blend of cinnamon and other spices as well as the caramelization of sugar during the baking process.

In the Boone brothers' time, families made speculoos mostly for special occasions like weddings, births, and St. Nicholas's Feast on the sixth of December. But why, wondered the brothers, should enjoyment of these cookies be limited to a few times every year? They opened their first bakery in 1932. Residents of Lembeke soon came to recognize the brothers' red truck as it drove around, delivering their freshly baked cookies door to door. Speculoos became a favorite in cafes all over Europe—in fact, every fifth cookie enjoyed in Belgium today is a speculoos or Biscoff.

Fast forward to 2007, when a prime-time television program in Belgium called *De Bedenkers* ("The Inventors") put out a call for entries. A culinary enthusiast and mother of three named Els Scheppers saw her chance. She entered—and ultimately became a show finalist—with the idea of making a spread from Biscoff cookies. The recipe she created has the consistency of peanut butter but is nut-free and vegan. It has since become one of the most popular products offered by Lotus Bakeries, the company descended from the Boone brothers' original bakery.

Next, we cross the ocean to Ohio, where a few years ago Katrina Bahl, an avid baker and a mother of two hungry boys, faced the possible end of one of her family's cherished holiday traditions. Her husband's family has made buckeyes for half a century, using a recipe passed down through the generations. Buckeyes are a smooth, dense peanut butter filling dipped in chocolate, to resemble the nut from Ohio's state tree. Katrina would sit with her mother-in-law and make hundreds of buckeyes each year—until she discovered that one of her sons had a peanut allergy.

For a year or so, it looked like this classic Ohio tradition would end for the Bahl family. Katrina tried various substitutes for buckeyes, including sunflower butter, but they just didn't taste right. And then, she says, "I tried making the buckeyes with Biscoff Spread. It worked! Now my son can be included in our family's tradition again."

Katrina went on to think up other uses of Biscoff spread and cookies, and began blogging about her creations. She developed a following—Biscoff lovers eager to incorporate its irresistible flavor into their own culinary creations, foodies from around the world. Before long, the idea for this cookbook was born.

In these pages, you'll find over 70 unique recipes, complete with photos and Katrina's insights into how they came to be. The sweet treats include cookies, cakes, frosting, quick breads, mousse, waffles, and other family favorites. "Many people love the snickerdoodles," Katrina reports, "especially hot out of the oven, when the spread in the middle oozes out when you bite in."

Now it's time for you to step in and become part of the Biscoff Cookie and Spread tradition. But first, a helpful tip from Katrina: "If you bring one of these desserts to a party or wine-tasting, be sure to bring a jar of Biscoff Spread with you, as I do! That way, when people say—as they inevitably will—'Wow, what's in that?' you'll be able to show them, and help them become fans themselves."

INTRODUCTION

My life changed on September 15, 2011. It was 9:30 AM, and my youngest son was safely strapped into his high chair while my oldest son was helping me make a fun treat. Nothing was unusual about the day. No one was being dangerous or careless. The three of us were happily going about our morning baking and eating, laughing and making a mess together in the kitchen. Then Timothy reached over from his high chair and swiped two pieces of cereal from Luke's bowl. We were making a dessert using a peanut butter cereal and Luke had been munching on the leftovers.

Never in my life will I forget the allergic reaction. It was fast and furious. Timothy's tiny face and neck turned red and swelled up with hives. I was terrified and helpless to protect my baby from this thing that was happening in his little body. After taking a few moments to note that he was not having difficulty breathing (thank God!), I called his pediatrician. You likely know the rest of the story. He is allergic to peanuts.

For the first few months after my son's initial reaction, I felt completely overwhelmed with the choices we had to make every minute of every day concerning the food that he consumed. But life goes on. My husband and I were diligent about educating ourselves and our family. Three years later, Timothy knows to double check with us if he has been offered food. Our home is completely nut-free. This book comes from a desire to adapt our favorite recipes so that they're safe for our whole family to enjoy together.

The great news is that Biscoff Spread isn't just for the person with peanut allergies! When I first brought Biscoff into our home, I had to do some convincing to get my husband to try this alternative to peanut butter that I was eating by the spoonful. One bite was all it took, and he became just as addicted as the rest of us. In fact, it's fair to say he's now the biggest Biscoff fan in our home, constantly raiding the cupboards in search of the next open jar. Every spoonful of the sweet, caramelized cookie butter tempts you to enjoy another bite. Biscoff cookies and spread lend the perfect flavor to your favorite desserts and sweet treats. I hope you enjoy baking from this book as well as coming up with your own Biscoff-inspired creations!

THE BISCOFF

COOKIE & SPREAD

COOKBOOK

BREAKFAST SWEETS

Easy Biscoff Granola, 2

Biscoff Yogurt Parfaits, 5

Biscoff Apple Sandwiches, 6

Biscoff Overnight Oats, 9

Buttermilk Biscoff Pancakes, 10

Quick Biscoff Waffles, 13

Biscoff Cheesecake-Stuffed French Toast, 14

Biscoff Biscotti, 17

Biscoff Cinnamon Rolls, 19

Biscoff Cream-Filled Donut Holes, 22

Easy Biscoff Granola

Granola is easy to make at home, and this Biscoff granola comes together quickly. Enjoy it served with milk or as a topping for your favorite yogurt. Try it served over waffles or in *Biscoff Yogurt Parfaits* (page 5).

YIELD: 2 cups

INGREDIENTS

½ cup Creamy or Crunchy Biscoff Spread

¼ cup honey

3 tablespoons brown sugar

2 cups old-fashioned oats

Cinnamon sugar (1 teaspoon ground cinnamon + 3 tablespoons granulated sugar), optional

Dried fruits, chocolate chips, nuts, or seeds, optional

INSTRUCTIONS

1. Preheat oven to 325°F. Line a baking sheet with parchment paper or a nonstick silicone baking mat. Don't skip this step—granola may stick to the bottom of your baking sheet and burn.

2. Microwave Biscoff Spread, honey, and brown sugar in a microwave-safe bowl for 30–60 seconds, or until creamy. Alternately, warm over medium-low heat on the stovetop, stirring constantly.

3. Pour wet ingredients over the oats in a large bowl. Mix and spread onto prepared baking sheet. Bake for 10 minutes; stir. Bake for another 8–10 minutes.

4. Sprinkle with cinnamon sugar when still warm if desired. Make a trail mix by adding your favorite mix-ins when the granola is completely cooled: raisins, dried cranberries, chopped Biscoff cookies, chocolate chips, and/or seeds.

5. Let cool completely before storing in an airtight container.

Biscoff Yogurt Parfaits

Layer these parfaits up with yogurt, granola, Biscoff cookie crumbles, and fresh berries—perfect for breakfast or an afternoon snack. Try it with *Easy Biscoff Granola* for double the Biscoff flavor!

YIELD: 4 servings

INGREDIENTS

1 cup Easy Biscoff Granola (page 2)

½ cup Biscoff cookies, coarsely crumbled

2 cups yogurt, any flavor

Fresh berries

INSTRUCTIONS

Mix granola with Biscoff cookie crumbles. Alternate layers of yogurt, granola mix, and berries in mini parfait glasses, dessert shot glasses, or wine glasses. Serve immediately.

Biscoff Apple Sandwiches

Who could resist these cute little apple sandwiches? Serve them for breakfast with some homemade *Easy Biscoff Granola* (page 2) or as an after-school snack. Slice the apples up and then let the kids make their own sandwiches!

YIELD: 4 sandwiches

INGREDIENTS

2 apples

2 teaspoons lemon juice, optional

½ cup Creamy or Crunchy Biscoff Spread

¼ cup granola, optional

¼ cup mini chocolate chips, optional

INSTRUCTIONS

1. Core apples and cut crosswise into 8 slices total.

2. If you are not going to be serving the sandwiches immediately, dip apple slices in lemon juice to keep the apple from browning.

3. Spread Creamy Biscoff Spread on 4 apple slices. Top with 4 apple slices that match in size.

4. Roll exposed sides in granola and/or chocolate chips if desired.

Biscoff Overnight Oats

Overnight oats are a great way to use up those last few scoops of Biscoff Spread in the bottom of your jar. Don't waste one drop! Simply pile all of the ingredients into the jar the night before and you'll wake up to a delicious breakfast before you even have a chance to turn on your coffee maker! If you want to enjoy these before you reach the bottom of the jar just be sure to choose a container with a lid. Feel free to customize this recipe as well. The general guideline is to have equal parts oats to liquid or yogurt; add more or less liquid if you prefer your oats thicker or thinner.

YIELD: 2 servings

INGREDIENTS

2-3 tablespoons Creamy or Crunchy Biscoff Spread

½ teaspoon vanilla extract

⅓ cup vanilla yogurt

½ cup milk

½ cup old-fashioned oats

1 tablespoon sugar, honey, or agave (adjust more or less to taste)

½ teaspoon ground cinnamon

2 tablespoons chocolate chips, optional

Fresh berries, optional

INSTRUCTIONS

1. Add all ingredients in a small jar with a lid. Stir or shake to combine.

2. Set in the refrigerator overnight. Top with fresh berries or chocolate chips before serving.

Children love shaking the jar and it's a perfect way to get them excited about trying new foods. They will wake up with excitement as they anticipate tasting their creation the next morning!

Get creative with add-ins: flax, coconut, dried fruit, crunchy granola, chia seeds. Or top with fresh jam to mimic a peanut butter and jelly taste.

Buttermilk Biscoff Pancakes

During the early years of our marriage we lived near a popular specialty breakfast restaurant that served the most amazing pancakes. The wait time on weekend mornings was almost always 45 minutes (sometimes longer!) to be seated. I didn't understand all the fuss about pancakes until I had finally eaten there. I never wanted to leave. These Biscoff pancakes are every bit as good as any that I would pay money for. Try them with *Biscoff Breakfast Syrup* (page 143).

YIELD: 4 servings

INGREDIENTS

1½ cups all-purpose flour

¼ cup brown sugar, packed

1½ teaspoons baking powder

½ teaspoon baking soda

½ teaspoon pumpkin pie spice (or ground cinnamon)

¼ cup buttermilk

½ cup Creamy Biscoff Spread

1 tablespoon canola or vegetable oil

1 tablespoon vanilla extract

2 eggs

INSTRUCTIONS

1. Whisk together flour, brown sugar, baking powder, baking soda, and pumpkin pie spice. Set aside.

2. In a large bowl or stand mixer fitted with a whisk attachment, whisk together the buttermilk, Biscoff Spread, oil, vanilla, and eggs.

3. Slowly add dry ingredients to the wet and stir just to combine, being careful not to overmix.

4. Heat griddle or skillet to medium heat. Pour batter onto griddle. Flip pancakes when the tops are covered in air bubbles and edges are set. Cook the other side until set. Serve immediately.

Quick Biscoff Waffles

I would be surprised if there are many waffle-haters out there. All of those little built-in syrup pockets are irresistible! These Quick Biscoff Waffles crisp up on the outside and are perfectly soft and tender inside. I rarely add extra butter when serving, but you can never go wrong with cold butter against a hot waffle. Be sure to try these with *Biscoff Breakfast Syrup* (page 143) and fresh berries!

    Yield and cook time will vary according to size and model of the waffle maker you are using. You can keep these warm in a 200°F oven on cookie sheets until you are ready to serve them all.

YIELD: 4 servings

INGREDIENTS

2 cups all-purpose flour

2 teaspoons baking powder

3 tablespoons granulated sugar

¼ teaspoon salt

⅓ cup Creamy Biscoff Spread

6 tablespoons butter, melted

2 eggs

1½ cups milk

½ teaspoon almond or vanilla extract

INSTRUCTIONS

1. In a small bowl sift together flour, baking powder, sugar, and salt. Set aside.

2. In the bowl of your mixer fitted with the whisk attachment, add Biscoff Spread, melted butter, eggs, milk, and almond extract. Mix on low to medium speed, and then slowly add the dry ingredients until just wet, being careful not to overmix.

3. Add batter to the waffle maker per the manufacturer's instructions, and cook until set up and golden.

Biscoff Cheesecake–Stuffed French Toast

When developing recipes I know I've nailed it if everyone at the table is sitting and eating in silence. As I peer into the dining room I can see my houseful of boys devouring their plates of food, all while keeping an eye on that last serving. This recipe was such a hit with my husband that he ate two and then grabbed another one to go on his way out the door.

YIELD: 4 servings

INGREDIENTS

4 oz cream cheese, softened

¼ cup brown sugar, packed

½ cup Creamy Biscoff Spread

8 slices bread

1 egg

1 cup milk

1 teaspoon vanilla extract

1 cup Biscoff cookies, crushed

Powdered sugar and syrup, optional

This would make the perfect special breakfast dish for a holiday morning or birthday celebration. Enjoy it on the weekend when you have time to savor every bite!

INSTRUCTIONS

1. Mix cream cheese and brown sugar in a small bowl.

2. Make 4 sandwiches by spreading 4 slices of bread with Biscoff Spread and topping with 4 slices of bread with cream cheese mixture. Set aside.

3. In a shallow dish whisk together egg, milk, and vanilla.

4. Spray griddle with nonstick cooking spray and heat to medium-low heat. Set up a dipping station with sandwiches, egg mixture, and crushed cookies. Dip each sandwich in the egg mixture to coat completely, then dip in cookie crumbs, pressing into both sides of the sandwich.

5. Cook over the griddle 2 minutes on each side until golden.

6. Dust with powdered sugar and serve with *Biscoff Breakfast Syrup* (page xxx) if desired.

Biscoff Biscotti

Biscoff cookies are delicious dipped in coffee for a sweet treat. It seemed only natural to create a crunchy Biscoff biscotti. The texture is firm with a crisp crust, perfect for enjoying alongside your coffee.

YIELD: 24 slices

INGREDIENTS

2 cups all-purpose flour

1 teaspoon baking powder

2 teaspoons pumpkin pie spice

½ teaspoon salt

3 eggs

1 egg yolk

¾ cup dark brown sugar, packed

½ cup Creamy Biscoff Spread

1 egg white

2 tablespoons granulated sugar

2 tablespoons white chocolate, optional

INSTRUCTIONS

1. Preheat oven to 350°F.

2. Whisk together flour, baking powder, pumpkin pie spice, and salt. Set aside.

3. In a large bowl using a handheld mixer or stand mixer fitted with a paddle attachment, beat eggs, egg yolk, and brown sugar. Add Biscoff Spread and mix until smooth. Slowly add the dry ingredients to the wet.

4. Divide dough into 2 equal portions and form 2 oval logs on a baking sheet lined with parchment paper or a silicone baking mat. Brush with egg white and sprinkle with sugar.

5. Bake for 25 minutes. Allow the loaves to cool on the baking sheet for 10–15 minutes. Move loaves to a cutting board and cut into approximately 24 slices. Transfer back to the baking sheets and bake at 300°F for 15 minutes.

6. Allow the cookies to cool on the baking sheet for 4 minutes and transfer to a wire rack to cool completely.

7. Drizzle with melted white chocolate if desired.

Biscoff Cinnamon Rolls

Cinnamon rolls are a bit of a traditional food. By that I mean families often enjoy cinnamon rolls as a tradition for special occasions like birthday breakfasts, holiday mornings, and the first day of school. I'm all for traditions, but I'm also all for spicing things up every once in a while. Once you try these rolls I think there's a good chance that you'll have your newest tradition. I've included instructions on how to prepare these the night before if you would like to enjoy them with little fuss in the morning. Just be sure to leave yourself an hour for them to rise before baking.

YIELD: 12 rolls

INGREDIENTS

FOR THE ROLLS

2½ cups all-purpose flour, divided + more for rolling

¼ cup granulated sugar

1 teaspoon salt

1 package instant yeast (2¼ teaspoons)

2 tablespoons butter

¼ cup milk

½ cup warm water (110–115°F.)

1 egg

FOR THE FILLING

6 tablespoons Creamy Biscoff Spread

¼ cup granulated sugar

1 tablespoon ground cinnamon

FOR THE GLAZE

1 cup powdered sugar

1 teaspoon vanilla extract

2 tablespoons milk or heavy cream

(CONTINUED ON PAGE 20)

1. Set aside ½ cup flour. Whisk together 2 cups flour, sugar, salt, and yeast. Set aside.

2. Melt butter in the microwave and add milk and warm water. Stir and use an instant-read thermometer to check the temperature, taking special care not to touch the bottom of the bowl (where glass could be hotter than the liquids inside). It should be between 110 and 115°F. Microwave the mixture longer or wait a few minutes to cool as necessary.

3. Stir the liquids into the flour mixture. Add the egg and the reserved flour. Keep stirring. (I use a sturdy wooden spoon.) Dough will be ready when it is smooth and elastic. Turn out onto a floured surface and knead for 3–5 minutes. Transfer to a large glass bowl that has been sprayed with cooking spray and let the dough rest for 8–10 minutes.

4. Roll the dough out in a large rectangle (about 15 × 8 inches). Place spoonfuls of Biscoff Spread all over the rectangle and spread to cover. Mix together the sugar and cinnamon and sprinkle it all over the Biscoff Spread. Roll up the dough tightly, lengthwise. Cut into 12 even pieces and place in a pie pan that has been sprayed with nonstick cooking spray.

5. If you're planning to let the rolls rise overnight, cover the pie plate with plastic wrap and set in the refrigerator. The next morning remove the rolls from the refrigerator and let rise for 1 hour.

6. If you're cooking them the same day, cover the rolls with plastic wrap and place in a warm spot free from drafts. Let rise until doubled, about 1 hour.

7. After 1 hour, preheat the oven to 375°F. Bake for 25–30 minutes until golden and cooked through. Check rolls after 15 minutes. If the tops are getting too dark, tent the pie plate with foil.

8. Mix the powdered sugar, vanilla, and milk together until smooth. Use more or less milk to achieve desired consistency. Use clear vanilla if you would like the glaze to remain pure white. Coat rolls with glaze before serving.

Biscoff Cream–Filled Donut Holes

There might not be anything better than homemade donuts. This is definitely a weekend recipe and is at a moderate level of difficulty because you have to move quickly and be mindful of the hot oil. Using a deep fryer takes out the guesswork with the oil temperature because it is calibrated to adjust the oil to a consistent temperature. It's all worth it in the end to bite into a sweet ball of fried dough filled with *Biscoff Cream Filling*.

YIELD: 30 donut holes

INGREDIENTS

FOR THE DONUTS

4–5 cups vegetable oil, for frying

2 cups all-purpose flour

2 tablespoons brown sugar, packed

4 teaspoons baking powder

½ teaspoon salt

1 cup milk

1 egg

¼ cup butter, melted and cooled

FOR THE CREAM FILLING

(see recipe on page 24)

FOR THE GLAZE

1 cup powdered sugar

2 tablespoons milk, optional

INSTRUCTIONS

FOR THE DONUTS

1. Fill a large skillet or heavy-bottomed pot with vegetable oil, about 2 inches deep. Using a deep-fry thermometer, heat oil to 350°F. Make sure it stays around that temperature each time you fry the dough. Alternately you can use a deep fryer set to 350°F.

2. In a large bowl using a handheld mixer or stand mixer fitted with a paddle attachment, mix flour, brown sugar, baking powder, and salt. Add milk and egg and mix for 1 minute until smooth. Then stir in the melted butter. Mix until a soft dough forms.

3. Check to be sure that your oil is at 350°F. Use a small cookie scoop to drop about tablespoon-sized dough balls into the hot oil, being sure to avoid hot oil spatters. Do not crowd the pot. I prefer to fry about 5 doughnut holes at a time.

4. Fry the doughnut holes for about 2 minutes, flipping halfway through, ensuring all sides are cooked through. Remove doughnuts using a long-armed slotted spoon. Drain on paper towels and allow to cool before filling.

(CONTINUED ON PAGE 25)

YIELD: 1½ cups

INGREDIENTS

½ cup butter, softened

¼ cup brown sugar, packed

½ cup Creamy Biscoff Spread

½ cup powdered sugar

3 tablespoons milk or cream

1. In a large bowl using a handheld mixer or stand mixer fitted with a paddle attachment, cream the butter, brown sugar, and Biscoff Spread for 2 minutes until light and fluffy.

2. Add powdered sugar, then thin out the filling with milk or cream to desired consistency.

3. Fill a piping bag fitted with a long, open metal tip with *Biscoff Cream Filling*. If you do not have a long tip then simply use a wooden skewer or small paring knife to poke a hole into the donut before filling.

The texture of this cream is slightly grainy due to the brown sugar. You can omit the brown sugar if a smoother cream is desired and replace with powdered sugar (¾ cup powdered sugar in total).

FOR THE GLAZE

If using glaze, mix together powdered sugar and milk. Dip tops of donuts into the simple glaze.

COOKIES

Biscoff Blossoms

This is a classic cookie recipe developed for my son, who has a peanut allergy. If you are making this for your friends or family members who have allergies, just be sure to choose a chocolate candy that you know is safe for their specific allergy. These soft, tender cookies are equally delicious without the chocolate center. We enjoy them both ways.

YIELD: 36 cookies

INGREDIENTS

1½ cups all-purpose flour

1 teaspoon baking soda

½ teaspoon salt

½ cup butter, softened

¾ cup Creamy Biscoff Spread

⅔ cup brown sugar, packed

1 egg

1 teaspoon vanilla extract

Granulated sugar

36 chocolate candies

INSTRUCTIONS

1. Whisk together flour, baking soda, and salt. Set aside.

2. In a large bowl using a handheld mixer or stand mixer fitted with a paddle attachment, cream butter, Biscoff Spread, and brown sugar for 2 minutes until light and fluffy.

3. Add egg and vanilla, followed by the dry ingredients. Mix well. Cover bowl with plastic wrap. Chill dough for at least 30 minutes, up to 1 hour.

4. Preheat oven to 375°F. Remove wrappers from chocolates.

5. Using a cookie scoop, shape dough into 1-inch balls and roll in granulated sugar. Place on an ungreased cookie sheet lined with parchment paper or a silicone baking mat. Bake for 8–10 minutes. Immediately press a chocolate into center of each cookie.

6. Allow the cookies to cool on the baking sheet for 4 minutes and transfer to a wire rack to cool completely.

To make prettier cookies, you can press a few chocolate chips into the tops of each dough ball before baking.

Biscoff Chocolate Chip Cookies

I used to be the most horrible chocolate chip cookie baker in all the land. I mean, my cookies were terrible, even inedible at times! You would think that years of failure would motivate me to improve, right? Nope! What finally motivated me was a *friendly* chocolate chip cookie competition at an annual family luau. Most of all I was motivated to beat my brother-in-law because he's very competitive and it drives him crazy when I win anything. My cookies beat Chad's and I'm happy to report that I came home with the trophy! We have both upped our culinary game through the years but I think I could still defeat him with these Biscoff Chocolate Chip Cookies.

YIELD: 30 cookies

INGREDIENTS

1½ cups all-purpose flour

¼ teaspoon baking soda

¼ teaspoon baking powder

¼ teaspoon ground cinnamon

¼ teaspoon salt

½ cup butter, softened

½ cup Creamy Biscoff Spread

¼ cup granulated sugar

½ cup brown sugar, packed

1 egg

1 teaspoon vanilla extract

1 cup milk chocolate chips

INSTRUCTIONS

1. Whisk together flour, baking soda, baking powder, cinnamon, and salt. Set aside.

2. In a large bowl using a handheld mixer or stand mixer fitted with a paddle attachment, cream butter, Biscoff Spread, and sugars for 2 minutes until light and fluffy.

3. Add egg and vanilla, followed by the dry ingredients. Mix until just combined. Fold in the chocolate chips. Cover bowl with plastic wrap. Chill dough for at least 30 minutes, up to 1 hour.

4. Using a cookie scoop, shape dough into 1-inch balls.

5. Place on an ungreased cookie sheet lined with parchment paper or a silicone baking mat. Bake for 8–10 minutes until golden around the edges.

6. Allow the cookies to cool on the baking sheet for 4 minutes and transfer to a wire rack to cool completely.

Biscoff Cloud Cookies

These cookies are puffy and super-soft. You will love the chewy texture, and you don't have to chill the dough before baking!

YIELD: 30 cookies

INGREDIENTS

½ cup unsalted butter, room temperature

⅓ cup Creamy Biscoff Spread

¾ cup brown sugar, packed

½ cup granulated sugar

1 egg

1 teaspoon vanilla extract

2 cups all-purpose flour

1 tablespoon cornstarch

½ teaspoon salt

½ teaspoon ground cinnamon

INSTRUCTIONS

1. Preheat oven to 350°F.

2. In the bowl of your mixer combine softened butter, Creamy Biscoff Spread, brown sugar, and granulated sugar at medium speed until combined.

3. Add egg and vanilla, and beat on low speed until ingredients are fully incorporated.

4. In a separate bowl combine flour, cornstarch, salt, and cinnamon.

5. Slowly add dry ingredients to the wet ingredients in the mixer. Mix until combined.

6. Drop by rounded tablespoon onto a silicone or parchment-lined cookie sheet. Bake for 8 minutes. Allow the cookies to cool on the baking sheet for 4 minutes and transfer to a wire rack to cool completely.

Biscoff Crisscross Cookies

I know you might not believe that these cookies have no butter, but they work! Try it! Enjoy the classic crisscross cookie in Biscoff form. These cookies crisp up on the outside with just enough crunch from the sugar while staying chewy and tender throughout. Enjoy them alongside a big glass of milk.

YIELD: 20 cookies

INGREDIENTS

1 cup all-purpose flour

¾ teaspoon baking soda

½ teaspoon baking powder

¼ teaspoon salt

1 cup Creamy Biscoff Spread

¾ cup brown sugar, packed

1 egg

1 teaspoon vanilla extract

Granulated sugar for coating

INSTRUCTIONS

1. Preheat oven to 350°F.

2. Whisk together flour, baking soda, baking powder, and salt. Set aside.

3. In a large bowl using a handheld mixer or stand mixer fitted with a paddle attachment, cream the Biscoff Spread and brown sugar for 2 minutes until light and fluffy.

4. Add egg and vanilla and mix until incorporated.

5. Slowly add the dry ingredients to the wet and mix until just combined. The dough will be stiff.

6. Using a cookie scoop, place rounded tablespoons into a shallow bowl filled with granulated sugar. Place on an ungreased cookie sheet lined with parchment paper or a silicone baking mat and use a fork to press down to make a criss-cross pattern.

7. Bake for 8–9 minutes. Allow the cookies to cool on the baking sheet for 4 minutes and transfer to a wire rack to cool completely.

Biscoff Cut-Out Cookies

Some of my earliest baking memories are of spending the day making a giant mess in the kitchen with my mom as we baked and decorated cut-out cookies. I wasn't a tidy little helper at all; I think it was somehow my goal to get flour onto every surface imaginable. I'm so grateful to have those memories spent with my mom today. She certainly knew how to make a fun childhood for her kids! These Biscoff cut-out cookies are the perfect way to spice up your normal holiday baking routine. They are perfect for fall baking as well. Dip them in *Biscoff Glaze* or frost with *Biscoff Buttercream* (page 26) for double the deliciousness!

YIELD: 30 cookies (depending on the size of your cookie cutters)

INGREDIENTS

3¼ cups all-purpose flour

2 teaspoons baking powder

1 teaspoon ground cinnamon

1 cup butter, softened

½ cup Creamy Biscoff Spread

½ cup granulated sugar

½ cup brown sugar, packed

1 egg

1 teaspoon vanilla extract

Biscoff Glaze (page 150) or other frosting

INSTRUCTIONS

1. Preheat oven to 350°F.

2. Whisk together flour, baking powder, and cinnamon. Set aside.

3. In a large bowl using a handheld mixer or stand mixer fitted with a paddle attachment, cream butter, Biscoff Spread, and sugars for 2 minutes until light and fluffy.

4. Add egg and vanilla and mix until incorporated.

5. Slowly add the dry ingredients to the wet ½ cup at a time and mix until just combined.

6. Lightly flour your workspace and roll out dough to about ¼ inch thickness. You may need to flour the rolling pin as well. Cut out cookies and place onto an ungreased cookie sheet lined with parchment paper or a silicone baking mat.

7. Bake for 6–8 minutes. Allow the cookies to cool on the baking sheet for 4 minutes and transfer to a wire rack to cool completely.

8. Dip cookies in *Biscoff Glaze* or frost with your favorite icing.

Biscoff No-Bake Cookies

This classic peanut butter no-bake cookie recipe gets a modern update with Biscoff Spread and cinnamon. Ugly food deserves a chance too! Didn't your mama tell you never to judge a book by its cover? Chewy and chocolaty, these cookies will remind you of your childhood. The hardest part is waiting for them to set up properly.

YIELD: 30 cookies

INGREDIENTS

½ cup butter, room temperature

1 cup granulated sugar

½ cup brown sugar, packed

Dash salt

½ teaspoon ground cinnamon

½ cup milk

½ cup Creamy Biscoff Spread

1 teaspoon vanilla extract

3 cups quick oats

INSTRUCTIONS

1. In a saucepan melt butter over medium heat.

2. Stir in granulated sugar, brown sugar, salt, ground cinnamon, and milk.

3. Continue stirring until mixture begins to boil. Lower temperature and boil 1 minute without stirring.

4. Remove from heat immediately and stir in Creamy Biscoff Spread, then vanilla extract, until smooth. Add quick oats and stir until incorporated.

5. Drop by heaping spoonful onto parchment paper or wax paper and allow to cool until set.

Biscoff Oatmeal Raisin Cookies

You'll love these soft, tender oatmeal cookies studded with raisins. Biscoff Spread adds a whole new layer of flavor in the background of this classic afternoon snack.

YIELD: 24 cookies

INGREDIENTS

1 cup all-purpose flour

½ teaspoon baking soda

½ teaspoon baking powder

½ teaspoon salt

½ cup butter, softened

½ cup Creamy Biscoff Spread

¼ cup granulated sugar

½ cup brown sugar, packed

1 egg

1 teaspoon vanilla extract

2 cups quick oats

½ cup raisins

INSTRUCTIONS

1. Preheat oven to 350°F.

2. Whisk together flour, baking soda, baking powder, and salt. Set aside.

3. In a large bowl using a handheld mixer or stand mixer fitted with a paddle attachment, cream butter, Biscoff Spread, and sugars for 2 minutes until light and fluffy.

4. Add egg and vanilla and mix until incorporated.

5. Slowly add the dry ingredients to the wet and mix until just combined. Stir in oats and raisins.

6. Drop by rounded tablespoon onto a silicone or parchment-lined cookie sheet. Bake for 8–10 minutes. Allow the cookies to cool on the baking sheet for 4 minutes and transfer to a wire rack to cool completely.

Butterscotch Biscoff Pudding Cookies

Pudding cookies are soft and chewy with a tender, soft texture and they stay fresh days later. Biscoff and butterscotch pair up perfectly in this cookie. Or feel free to swap out chocolate pudding and chocolate chips (or vanilla and white chocolate chips) for an equally delicious version. Mix and match—you can't go wrong!

YIELD: 36 cookies

INGREDIENTS

1 small (3.4 oz) box butterscotch pudding mix

2½ cups all-purpose flour

1 teaspoon baking powder

½ cup butter, softened

½ cup Creamy Biscoff Spread

½ cup brown sugar, packed

¼ cup granulated sugar

2 eggs

1 teaspoon vanilla extract

1½ cups butterscotch chips

INSTRUCTIONS

1. Whisk together pudding mix, flour, and baking soda. Set aside.

2. In a large bowl using a handheld mixer or stand mixer fitted with a paddle attachment, cream the butter, Biscoff Spread, and sugars for 2 minutes until light and fluffy.

3. Add eggs one at a time and vanilla and mix until incorporated.

4. Slowly add the dry ingredients to the wet and mix until just combined. Fold in butterscotch chips.

5. Cover bowl with plastic wrap. Chill dough for at least 30 minutes.

6. Preheat oven to 350°F.

7. Using a cookie scoop, place rounded table-spoons on an ungreased cookie sheet lined with parchment paper or a silicone baking mat.

8. Bake for 7–9 minutes. Allow the cookies to cool on the baking sheet for 4 minutes and transfer to a wire rack to cool completely.

White Chocolate Biscoff Cookies

You will love these giant Biscoff cookies stuffed with white chocolate! Sweet white chocolate pairs so well with the spiced Biscoff Spread. Enjoy them warm straight from the oven with a cold glass of milk.

YIELD: 36 large cookies

INGREDIENTS

1¾ cups all-purpose flour

2 teaspoons baking powder

½ teaspoon salt

½ cup unsalted butter, softened

½ cup granulated sugar

¾ cup light brown sugar, packed

¾ cup Creamy Biscoff Spread

1 egg

1 teaspoon vanilla extract

½ cup white chocolate chips or discs

Additional sugar for coating

INSTRUCTIONS

1. Whisk together flour, baking powder, and salt. Set aside.

2. In a large bowl using a handheld mixer or stand mixer fitted with a paddle attachment, cream together the butter, sugars, and Biscoff Spread for 2 minutes until light and fluffy.

3. Add egg and vanilla to the mixer. Then slowly incorporate the dry ingredients. Dough will be wet. Cover bowl with plastic wrap. Chill dough for at least 30 minutes, up to 1 hour.

4. Preheat oven to 350°F.

5. Using a cookie scoop, form dough into 2-tablespoon balls and flatten slightly into discs. Place a few pieces of white chocolate on top and cover with another disc of dough. Pinch seams to seal and roll in sugar.

6. Place on an ungreased cookie sheet lined with parchment paper or a silicone baking mat. Leave plenty of room for spreading. Bake for 12–15 minutes depending on the size of dough balls you formed.

Biscoff-Stuffed Snickerdoodles

These cookies. THESE COOKIES! I just can't even describe how amazingly delicious they are—perfectly puffy, soft, chewy, and oozing with Biscoff Spread. My sister-in-law was completely smitten with them. I think her exact words were, "Katrina! These cookies are insanely amazing. They are way too good to be true. In fact, they should be illegal."

YIELD: 18 large cookies

INGREDIENTS

3 cups all-purpose flour

1 teaspoon baking soda

2 teaspoons ground cinnamon

¼ teaspoon salt

2 teaspoons cream of tartar

1 cup butter, softened

1 cup granulated sugar

1 egg

1 teaspoon vanilla extract

½ cup Creamy Biscoff Spread

Cinnamon sugar (⅓ cup granulated sugar + 2 teaspoons ground cinnamon)

These cookies are *very large* and it may be difficult to gauge doneness. Mine have almost always come out at 10 minutes, but possibly 12 minutes for the first batch.

INSTRUCTIONS

1. Preheat oven to 375°F.

2. Whisk together flour, baking soda, cinnamon, salt, and cream of tartar. Set aside.

3. In a large bowl using a handheld mixer or stand mixer fitted with a paddle attachment, cream butter and sugar for 2 minutes until light and fluffy.

4. Add egg and vanilla and mix until incorporated.

5. Slowly add the dry ingredients to the wet and mix until just combined.

6. Using a cookie scoop, place 6 rounded tablespoons on an ungreased cookie sheet lined with parchment paper or a silicone baking mat. Gently press dough down into discs. Top with approximately 1 teaspoon Biscoff Spread, then another disc of cookie dough. Pinch the seam with your fingers to seal in the Biscoff Spread. Roll in cinnamon sugar and return to baking sheet.

7. Bake for 10–12 minutes. Allow the cookies to cool on the baking sheet for 4 minutes and transfer to a wire rack to cool completely. Sprinkle each cookie with more cinnamon sugar if desired.

BARS & BROWNIES

Chocolate Biscoff Shortbread Squares

The only thing better than a buttery shortbread is a buttery shortbread topped with a beautiful chocolate Biscoff swirl. These *Chocolate Biscoff Shortbread Squares* are sure to impress!

YIELD: 24 squares

INGREDIENTS

1⅓ cups butter, softened and cubed

½ cup granulated sugar

2½ cups all-purpose flour

2 cups milk chocolate chips

¼ cup + 3 tablespoons Creamy Biscoff Spread, divided

These shortbread squares are equally delicious when prepared with white chocolate instead of milk chocolate.

INSTRUCTIONS

1. Preheat oven to 350°F.

2. Line a 9 x 13-inch baking dish with aluminum foil or parchment paper, leaving at least 1 inch hanging over the sides. Spray with nonstick cooking spray.

3. In a large bowl use a pastry blender to mix together butter, sugar, and flour until crumbly. Gather the dough and press into prepared pan. Pierce all over with a fork.

4. Bake 20 minutes and allow to cool at least 20 minutes.

5. In a microwave-safe bowl melt chocolate for 30–60 seconds. Stir and return to microwave for 30–60 more seconds until melted. Stir in ¼ cup Biscoff Spread.

6. Pour chocolate over the shortbread. Heat 3 tablespoons Biscoff Spread in the microwave for 15 seconds. Drizzle over the chocolate and use a butter knife to swirl around for a marbled look. Let set up and cool completely before cutting.

Fudgy Biscoff Swirl Brownies

There will always be those who argue over whether cakelike brownie recipes are best or fudgelike brownie recipes have an advantage. Meanwhile I'll be in the corner eating all the brownies. I mean, seriously—must we argue over brownies? These fudgy brownies are thick and rich. The Biscoff swirl makes them so beautiful, too! Try them with some creamy vanilla ice cream, or cut up into a *Butterscotch Biscoff Trifle* (page 136).

YIELD: 24 brownies

INGREDIENTS

1 cup brown sugar, packed

½ cup granulated sugar

2 cups chocolate chips, milk or semi-sweet

½ cup butter

4 eggs

2 teaspoons vanilla extract

½ teaspoon salt

1 cup all-purpose flour

½ to 1 cup Creamy Biscoff Spread

INSTRUCTIONS

1. Preheat oven to 325°F.

2. Line a 9 x 13-inch baking dish with aluminum foil or parchment paper, leaving at least 1 inch hanging over the sides. Spray with nonstick cooking spray.

3. Place both sugars into the bowl of your mixer. Set aside.

4. Melt chocolate and butter over low heat. (Alternately you could do this step in the microwave in a microwave-safe bowl. Melt the chocolate in 30-second intervals and stir in between. Add butter and stir until melted completely.)

5. Remove from heat and pour into the bowl of your mixer with sugar and begin mixing on low speed. Add eggs, vanilla, and salt.

6. Add flour ½ cup at a time until fully incorporated.

7. Pour into prepared 9 x 13-inch pan.

8. Melt Creamy Biscoff Spread in a microwave-safe bowl for 15–30 seconds. Pour over the pan in 3 strips lengthwise. Run a butter knife through the batter the opposite direction (widthwise) to create swirls.

9. Bake 35–40 minutes until a toothpick placed in the center comes out clean.

Gooey Caramel Biscoff Brownies

These are my absolute favorite brownie base! It took me many years to develop this recipe that my family now loves. I was a boxed-brownie-mix girl through and through until I finally got this recipe perfect. I love that these brownies use simple pantry ingredients and come together almost as quickly as a box mix. The Biscoff layer gets a little help from a jar of caramel ice cream topping—*so* amazing!

YIELD: 12 brownies

INGREDIENTS

½ cup Creamy Biscoff Spread

½ cup caramel ice cream topping

1 cup butter

2 cups granulated sugar

3 eggs

3 teaspoons vanilla extract

⅔ cup cocoa powder

½ teaspoon baking powder

½ teaspoon salt

1 cup all-purpose flour

INSTRUCTIONS

1. Preheat oven to 325°F.

2. Line an 8 x 8-inch baking dish with aluminum foil or parchment paper, leaving at least 1 inch hanging over the sides. Spray with nonstick cooking spray.

3. Whisk together Biscoff Spread and caramel topping. Set aside.

4. In a medium saucepan over medium heat, melt butter. Remove from heat and add sugar; stir to combine. Beat in eggs and vanilla until combined.

5. Mix in cocoa, baking powder, and salt. Add flour and stir until just combined. Batter will be thick. Pour in enough batter to just cover the bottom of your prepared pan (approximately 1 cup) and spread into an even layer.

6. Pour caramel filling, and then top with the remaining brownie batter.

7. Bake 25–30 minutes until a toothpick placed in the center comes out clean. Let cool completely before cutting and serving.

No-Bake Biscoff Bars

These taste like giant peanut butter cups, except made with Biscoff. I've been making them since I was a child and I never tire of them.

YIELD: 16 bars

INGREDIENTS

BOTTOM LAYER

1 cup butter

1 cup Creamy Biscoff Spread

2 teaspoons vanilla extract

2 cups Biscoff cookie crumbs

2 cups powdered sugar

TOP LAYER

1¼ cups milk chocolate chips

¼ cup Creamy Biscoff Spread

Crushed Biscoff cookies for garnish, optional

This recipe can also be made in a 9 x 13-inch pan; it will just result in a thinner bar.

INSTRUCTIONS

1. Line a 9 x 9-inch baking dish with aluminum foil or parchment paper, leaving at least 1 inch hanging over the sides. Spray with nonstick cooking spray.

2. Prepare bottom layer: In a medium saucepan melt butter and Biscoff Spread, stirring constantly until smooth. Remove from heat.

3. Add vanilla, cookie crumbs, and powdered sugar. Stir again until combined.

4. Pour mixture into prepared pan.

5. Prepare top layer: Heat chocolate chips in a microwave-safe bowl for 30-second intervals until melted. Immediately stir in Biscoff Spread and stir until smooth. Pour evenly over bottom layer. Sprinkle with cookie crumbs if desired.

6. Refrigerate 20 minutes until set.

White Chocolate Biscoff Blondies

These dense bars are packed with sweet white chocolate flavor. The melted butter gives them their signature rich blondie taste. These are best enjoyed warm with a heaping scoop of ice cream topped with a warm Biscoff Spread drizzle.

YIELD: 8 slices

INGREDIENTS

2¼ cups all-purpose flour

½ teaspoon baking powder

½ teaspoon salt

1½ cups butter, melted and cooled

½ cup Creamy or Crunchy Biscoff Spread

1 cup brown sugar, packed

½ cup granulated sugar

1 egg plus 1 egg yolk

2 teaspoons vanilla extract

1½ cups white chocolate chips

INSTRUCTIONS

1. Preheat oven to 350°F. Grease a shallow tart or pie pan with nonstick cooking spray. Set aside.

2. In a small bowl whisk together flour, baking powder, and salt. Set aside.

3. In a large bowl using a handheld mixer or stand mixer fitted with a paddle attachment, cream the butter, Biscoff Spread, and sugars for 2 minutes until light and fluffy. Slowly add eggs and vanilla.

4. Slowly add the dry ingredients to the wet ingredients. Mix on low speed until just combined. Fold in white chocolate chips.

5. Press into the bottom of the prepared tart or pie pan. Bake for 15–18 minutes until a toothpick placed in the center comes out clean. This dish can be served warm if desired. Let set up and cool for at least 15 minutes before cutting and serving.

Biscoff-Bottomed Sugar Cookie Bars

As you can imagine, I am always developing new recipes and testing them so it's not often that a dessert gets repeated in our home. Classic sugar cookie bars, however, are my go-to dessert to feed a crowd. Top with your favorite frosting and sprinkles.

YIELD: 16–24 bars

INGREDIENTS

30 Biscoff cookies

4½ cups all-purpose flour

1 teaspoon salt

½ teaspoon baking soda

1 cup butter, softened

1 cup granulated sugar

1 cup brown sugar, packed

4 large eggs

2 teaspoons vanilla extract

Biscoff Buttercream (page 144) or other frosting, optional

Sprinkles/candies, optional, for decoration

INSTRUCTIONS

1. Preheat oven to 375°F.

2. Line a 9 × 13-inch baking dish with aluminum foil or parchment paper, leaving at least 1 inch hanging over the sides. Spray with nonstick cooking spray. Line the bottom of the pan with whole Biscoff cookies.

3. In a medium bowl sift together flour, salt, and baking soda. Set aside.

4. In a large bowl using a handheld mixer or stand mixer fitted with a paddle attachment, cream the butter and sugars for 2 minutes until light and fluffy. Add eggs one at a time followed by vanilla.

5. Slowly add the dry ingredients to the wet ingredients. Mix on low speed until just combined and dough is dense like sugar-cookie dough.

6. Using a cookie scoop or 2 spoons, place heaping piles of dough on the Biscoff cookies in the pan. Press the dough down until smooth and even.

7. Bake 13–15 minutes until a toothpick placed in the center comes out clean. Let cool completely before cutting and serving. Frost with *Biscoff Buttercream*, and top with decorations.

I wanted to incorporate the delicious taste of Biscoff and I think you will love the additional layer of flavor.

Honey-Oat Biscoff Bars

A generous amount of honey binds together the perfect combination of oats and crispy rice cereal. These no-bake granola bars are perfect for lunchboxes or an after school snack. Make some over the weekend to munch on all week . . . if they last that long.

YIELD: 9–12 bars

INGREDIENTS

2 cups quick oats

2 cups crispy rice cereal

Dash salt

½ teaspoon ground cinnamon

½ cup Creamy or Crunchy Biscoff Spread

½ cup honey

¼ cup brown sugar

½ teaspoon vanilla extract

INSTRUCTIONS

1. Line an 8 × 8-inch baking dish with aluminum foil or parchment paper, leaving at least 1 inch hanging over the sides. Spray with nonstick cooking spray.

2. In a medium bowl combine quick oats, crispy rice cereal, salt, and cinnamon. Set aside.

3. In a microwave-safe bowl melt Biscoff Spread and honey for 30 seconds. Stir and repeat if necessary. Stir in brown sugar and vanilla. Return to microwave for 30–60 more seconds. Stir and pour over dry ingredients.

4. Mix well (you may have to use your hands) until incorporated. Pour into prepared dish and press down. Allow to set up for at least 1 hour.

5. Using the aluminum foil overhang, lift bars from dish and cut into 9–12 servings.

Biscoff Marshmallow Cereal Treat Bars

There's nothing simple or average about these treats. Made with marshmallows *and* Marshmallow Fluff, these treats are extraordinary. Your family and friends will be coming back for more and begging you for the recipe!

YIELD: 16 bars

INGREDIENTS

¼ cup butter

⅓ cup Creamy Biscoff Spread

7 oz jar Marshmallow Fluff

10 oz marshmallows (approximately 40 large)

5 cups crispy rice cereal

This recipe can be prepared in a 9 x 13-inch dish. The resulting bar will just be thinner.

INSTRUCTIONS

1. Line a 9 x 9-inch baking dish with aluminum foil or parchment paper, leaving at least 1 inch hanging over the sides. Spray with nonstick cooking spray.

2. Place cereal in a large bowl. Set aside.

3. Heat butter, Biscoff Spread, and Marshmallow Fluff over low to medium heat on stovetop, stirring constantly until melted and heated through. Add marshmallows and continue to stir constantly until melted and incorporated.

4. Transfer to bowl and stir into cereal. Press down into prepared baking dish using greased hands that have been sprayed with nonstick cooking spray. Let set up for at least 30 minutes.

5. Lift out of pan and cut into 16 even pieces. Store in an airtight container.

Biscoff Tiramisu

Tiramisu is my husband's all-time favorite dessert. If it's on the menu he will choose it every time. In this version Biscoff cookies take the place of ladyfingers, and the cream is made up of a vanilla Biscoff pudding.

YIELD: 9 slices

INGREDIENTS

2 large (5.1 oz) packages vanilla pudding

½ cup Creamy Biscoff Spread

4 cups milk

¼ teaspoon ground cinnamon

6 oz espresso or dark-roast coffee

36 Biscoff cookies

1 teaspoon cocoa powder

This dessert has to be well chilled to cut a clean slice from the pan. You may wish to serve it up by using a large spoon or spatula instead. Sometimes for this dessert I suggest lining the baking dish with aluminum foil or parchment paper, leaving at least 1 inch hanging over the sides. Run a butter knife around the edge of the pan and use the overhang to carefully lift the dessert out. Cut into slices and serve.

INSTRUCTIONS

1. In a large bowl using a handheld mixer or stand mixer fitted with a paddle attachment, combine pudding mix, Biscoff Spread, and milk. Stir for 2 minutes and let set up in the refrigerator while you prepare the first cookie layer of the tiramisu.

2. Stir cinnamon into the coffee and pour into a shallow bowl. Dip approximately 18 cookies into coffee mixture and lay them in the bottom of a 9 x 9-inch square pan.

3. Spoon 2½ cups of filling over the cookies. Alternately you can place the filling into a large resealable plastic bag. Seal the bag and cut a hole in the corner. Force the filling through the hole.

4. Repeat with a second layer of cookies dipped in coffee and more filling. Dust with cocoa powder.

5. Let set up and chill in the refrigerator for at least 2 hours.

CAKES & CUPCAKES

Biscoff Applesauce Cake, 70

Biscoff Carrot Cake, 73

Biscoff Buckeye Cake, 74

Biscoff Coffee Cake with Biscoff Crumb Topping, 77

Biscoff Cookies-and-Cream Cupcakes, 80

Biscoff Custard Cake, 83

Biscoff No-Bake Cheesecake, 84

Biscoff Sheet Cake, 86

Biscoff Truffle Mousse Cheesecake, 89

Chocolate Espresso Biscoff Cupcakes, 92

Biscoff Applesauce Cake

Applesauce cake like Grandma used to make! You'll love this moist cake made with cinnamon applesauce and Creamy Biscoff Spread. There are even some old-fashioned oats tucked away in there.

YIELD: 8 servings

INGREDIENTS

FOR THE CAKE

1¼ cups cinnamon applesauce

1 cup old-fashioned oats

1½ cups all-purpose flour

1 teaspoon baking soda

½ teaspoon ground cinnamon

½ teaspoon ground nutmeg

¼ teaspoon salt

½ cup butter, softened

½ cup Creamy Biscoff Spread

1 cup granulated sugar

1 teaspoon vanilla extract

2 eggs

FOR THE CREAM CHEESE FROSTING

¼ cup butter, softened

4 oz cream cheese, softened

2 cups powdered sugar

1 teaspoon vanilla extract

INSTRUCTIONS

1. Heat applesauce to boiling over medium-high heat. Stir in oats and let cool 20 minutes.

2. Preheat oven to 350°F. Spray a deep 9-inch pie pan (or cake pan) with nonstick cooking spray.

3. Whisk together flour, baking soda, cinnamon, nutmeg and salt. Set aside.

4. In a large bowl using a handheld mixer or stand mixer fitted with a paddle attachment, cream the butter, Biscoff Spread, and sugar until light and fluffy. Add vanilla and eggs, followed by the applesauce mixture until just combined. Add the dry ingredients to the wet, being careful not to overmix. Pour into prepared pie pan.

5. Bake 40–50 minutes until a toothpick inserted in center comes out clean.

6. To make the frosting, in a large bowl using a handheld mixer or stand mixer fitted with a paddle attachment, beat the butter and cream cheese. Add powdered sugar and vanilla and beat until smooth.

Biscoff Carrot Cake

My mom took this cake to work with her one day and it got rave reviews from everyone! Even people who don't typically like carrot cake love this Biscoff version. It is moist without being too oily, and dense without being too rich. The *Biscoff Cream Cheese Frosting* really makes this cake shine.

YIELD: 10-12 servings

INGREDIENTS

2½ cups all-purpose flour

1 teaspoon baking powder

1 teaspoon baking soda

1 teaspoon pumpkin pie spice

¼ teaspoon allspice

¼ teaspoon nutmeg

½ teaspoon salt

4 large carrots, grated (approximately 2 cups)

½ cup Creamy Biscoff Spread

1½ cups granulated sugar

½ cup brown sugar, packed

3 eggs

¾ cup canola or vegetable oil

¾ cup Greek yogurt, plain

Biscoff Cream Cheese Frosting (page 157)

20 Biscoff cookies, plus crushed cookies for garnish

INSTRUCTIONS

1. Preheat oven to 350°F. Spray two 9-inch round cake pans with nonstick cooking spray.

2. Whisk together the flour, baking powder, baking soda, pumpkin pie spice, allspice, nutmeg, and salt. Toss dry ingredients with the grated carrot in a large bowl.

3. In a large bowl using a handheld mixer or stand mixer fitted with a paddle attachment, cream the Biscoff Spread, sugars, eggs, oil, and yogurt. Add carrot mixture and stir just until combined. Pour batter into prepared cake pans and bake for 30–40 minutes until a toothpick inserted into cake comes out clean. Cool cakes for 10 minutes, then remove to a wire rack to cool completely.

4. Frost the cake with *Biscoff Cream Cheese Frosting*. Line the edge of the cake with Biscoff cookies, plus a few more crushed on the top. Keep cake covered and refrigerated.

Biscoff Buckeye Cake

For me the hardest part of baking a cake is frosting and decorating it. I enjoy making the cake and making the frosting but my decorating skills are not terribly advanced. This cake solves that problem because the frosting is tucked away inside the cake beneath a layer of ganache. The end result is quite stunning and it comes together so easily. You can use your favorite boxed cake mix if you want to make it even simpler. Your secret is safe with me!

YIELD: 1 cake

INGREDIENTS

FOR THE CAKE

1½ cups all-purpose flour

⅔ cup unsweetened cocoa powder

1½ teaspoons baking powder

1 teaspoon baking soda

½ teaspoon salt

10 tablespoons unsalted butter, softened

1½ cups granulated sugar

1 cup buttermilk

3 eggs

2 teaspoons vanilla extract

INSTRUCTIONS

FOR THE CAKE

1. Preheat oven to 350°F. Spray two 9-inch round cake pans with nonstick cooking spray.

2. Whisk together flour, cocoa powder, baking powder, baking soda and salt in a medium bowl. Set aside.

3. In a large bowl using a handheld mixer or stand mixer fitted with a paddle attachment, cream the butter and sugar until fluffy and lighter in color. Slowly add buttermilk, eggs, and vanilla. Add the dry ingredients ½ cup at a time to the wet ingredients in your mixer bowl until incorporated, about 2 minutes.

4. Divide batter between prepared cake pans. Bake for 30–35 minutes until a toothpick inserted into cake comes out clean. Cool cakes for 10 minutes, then remove to a wire rack to cool completely.

(CONTINUED ON PAGE 76)

FOR THE FILLING

1 cup butter, softened

½ cup Creamy Biscoff Spread

4 cups powdered sugar, divided

¼ cup heavy cream (or milk)

2 teaspoons vanilla extract

1. In a large bowl using a handheld mixer or stand mixer fitted with a paddle attachment, cream butter and Biscoff Spread until smooth and fluffy (about 4 minutes).

2. Slowly add 2 cups of powdered sugar.

3. Pour in heavy cream or milk and vanilla.

4. Gradually incorporate the final 2 cups of the powdered sugar.

5. Mix on low speed until all ingredients are smooth and mixed well.

FOR THE GLAZE

14 oz sweetened condensed milk

1 cup dark chocolate chips

3 tablespoons Creamy Biscoff Spread

1 teaspoon vanilla extract

1. In a saucepan over medium heat combine the condensed milk, chocolate chips, and Biscoff Spread. Stir constantly until the chocolate chips are melted and the mixture is smooth. Do not allow to come to a boil.

2. Remove from heat and stir in vanilla. Let set for a few minutes while you assemble the cake. If the mixture gets too cool you can heat it up again just before pouring over the cake.

ASSEMBLE THE CAKE

1. Level cake rounds and place bottom layer on a large plate or cake stand. Spread center filling (it will be a thick layer). Top with the second cake round.

2. Pour glaze over the top of the cake, letting it run down the sides.

Biscoff Coffee Cake with Biscoff Crumb Topping

I love my job. I love developing recipes and sharing them with the world on my blog. One of my favorite things about it is the connection I get to have with my readers. People leave comments, or e-mail me questions, and they send me pictures of their versions of my dishes—I *love* that! Believe it or not, one of the most common questions I get asked is about a coffee cake recipe I have on the site. Many (so many!) people ask why coffee is not listed as an ingredient in my coffee cake, and why would I call it a coffee cake? People get really angry about this deception! Let's all just take a moment to remember that coffee cake is meant to be enjoyed *with* coffee. It isn't necessarily made of coffee. I love my job (I really do!).

YIELD: 16 servings

INGREDIENTS

FOR THE TOPPING

2½ cups all-purpose flour

½ cup Biscoff cookies, crushed

1 cup brown sugar, packed

½ cup granulated sugar

2 teaspoons cinnamon

½ teaspoon salt

1 cup butter, melted

FOR THE CAKE

2 cups all-purpose flour

1 teaspoon ground cinnamon

1 teaspoon baking soda

½ teaspoon salt

½ cup unsalted butter, softened

½ cup Creamy Biscoff Spread

1½ cups brown sugar, packed

2 eggs

1 teaspoon vanilla extract

1 cup Greek yogurt

(CONTINUED ON PAGE 79)

FOR THE TOPPING

1. Combine the flour with crushed Biscoff cookies. Set aside

2. In a medium bowl, whisk together sugars, cinnamon, and salt. Stir in melted butter, then add flour mixture. Stir with a fork until large crumbs form.

3. Put the topping in the refrigerator while preparing the cake.

FOR THE CAKE

1. Preheat oven to 350°F. Line a 9 × 13-inch baking dish with aluminum foil or parchment paper, leaving at least 1 inch hanging over the sides. Spray with nonstick cooking spray.

2. Whisk together flour, cinnamon, baking soda, and salt. Set aside.

3. In a large bowl using a handheld mixer or stand mixer fitted with a paddle attachment, cream butter, Biscoff Spread, and brown sugar 2 minutes until light and fluffy. Beat in eggs, one at a time, and vanilla until combined.

4. Slowly add Greek yogurt and dry ingredients alternately in 3 parts until incorporated. Scoop the batter evenly into prepared baking dish. Sprinkle with crumb topping.

5. Bake for 30–35 minutes until a toothpick placed in the center comes out clean.

Biscoff Cookies-and-Cream Cupcakes

Cookies and cream is one of the most enjoyed flavor combinations of all time. Why should the *other* cookie have all the fun? You'll love the simple sweetness of this vanilla cupcake studded with crushed Biscoff cookies and topped with a classic confectioners' frosting.

YIELD: 12 cupcakes

INGREDIENTS

FOR THE CUPCAKES

1½ cups cake flour

1½ teaspoons baking powder

¼ teaspoon salt

½ cup butter, softened

1 cup granulated sugar

2 eggs

½ cup milk

1 teaspoon vanilla extract

10 Biscoff cookies, crushed

FOR THE FROSTING

½ cup butter, softened

1 teaspoon vanilla extract

2 cups powdered sugar

2 tablespoons milk or cream

INSTRUCTIONS

FOR THE CUPCAKES

1. Preheat oven to 350°F. Line a muffin tin with 24 paper liners or coat generously with nonstick cooking spray.

2. Whisk together flour, baking powder, and salt in a medium bowl. Set aside.

3. In a large bowl using a handheld mixer or stand mixer fitted with a paddle attachment, cream the butter and sugar until fluffy and lighter in color. Add eggs one at a time followed by milk and vanilla. Add the dry ingredients ½ cup at a time to the wet ingredients in your mixer bowl until incorporated, about 1–2 minutes. Fold in crushed Biscoff cookies.

4. Spoon batter into prepared tin, filling ¾ full. Bake for 15–18 minutes until a toothpick inserted into cupcake comes out clean. Cool cupcakes on a wire rack.

FOR THE FROSTING

1. In a large bowl using a handheld mixer or stand mixer fitted with a paddle attachment, beat the butter until smooth and lighter in color, about 1 minute.

2. Add vanilla and powdered sugar and mix on low until incorporated. Add up to 2 tablespoons milk or cream to reach desired consistency. Turn mixer to medium-high speed and beat for 3 minutes until light and fluffy.

Biscoff Custard Cake

This cake separates into layers as it bakes and is so pretty when served. It's not overly sweet but it is thick and rich. Enjoy with fresh berries and fresh sweet cream.

YIELD: 9 squares

INGREDIENTS

4 eggs, room temperature

1 tablespoon water

1 cup brown sugar, packed

½ teaspoon salt

¼ cup Creamy Biscoff Spread

½ cup butter, softened

1 tablespoon vanilla extract

¾ cup all-purpose flour

2 cups milk

INSTRUCTIONS

1. Preheat oven to 325°F. Coat an 8 × 8-inch square baking dish with nonstick spray and set aside.

2. Separate the egg whites from the yolks. Be sure that no yolk gets into the whites. In a very clean, cold bowl of your electric mixer, beat the egg whites to stiff peaks with the whisk attachment. This will take several minutes on high speed. Transfer to a separate bowl and set aside.

3. Beat the egg yolks, water, brown sugar, and salt until the mixture becomes a light golden color. Add Biscoff Spread, butter, and vanilla and mix until smooth and combined.

4. Gradually add the flour. Mix and slowly start adding the milk. This will make the batter very thin and watery. This is fine.

5. Gently fold in the egg whites.

6. Pour batter into prepared baking dish and bake 1 hour or until the top is golden and does not jiggle.

7. Remove from oven and let cool completely. The cake will shrink in a little bit from the sides of the pan while cooling. Transfer to the refrigerator to chill before serving. Best served and stored cold.

Biscoff No-Bake Cheesecake

No-bake cheesecakes are the perfect summer treat. They're quick and delicious; what's not to love? Making a layered no-bake cheesecake is simple and one of my favorite tricks. You can use a store-bought graham cracker crust or make a homemade Biscoff cookie crust.

YIELD: 8 servings

INGREDIENTS

FOR THE CRUST

1½ cups finely crushed Biscoff cookies (24 cookies)

¼ cup brown sugar, packed

7 tablespoons butter, melted

FOR THE CHEESECAKE

8 oz cream cheese, softened

14 oz sweetened condensed milk

1 cup sour cream

¾ cup Creamy Biscoff Spread

Graham cracker piecrust

2 cups nondairy whipped topping, divided

8 Biscoff cookies, crumbled

INSTRUCTIONS

FOR THE CRUST

Combine cookie crumbs with sugar. Add butter and stir until mixed. Press into the bottom of a pie plate. Chill for 45 minutes to 1 hour before filling, in order to give the crust time to set.

FOR THE CHEESECAKE

1. In a large bowl using a handheld mixer or stand mixer fitted with a paddle attachment, beat the cream cheese for 2 minutes. Add condensed milk and sour cream and mix until smooth. Remove 2 cups of the batter and set aside. Add Biscoff Spread and mix again until smooth. Pour into the bottom of your piecrust.

2. Take the reserved batter and mix with nondairy whipped topping. Spoon over the bottom layer of the pie. Refrigerate at least 2 hours until ready to serve. Keep refrigerated.

3. Sprinkle with cookie crumbles before serving.

Biscoff Sheet Cake

Sheet cakes are an easy, no-fuss way to serve dessert to a crowd. This Biscoff version is a modern twist on the classic Texas sheet cake. It melts in your mouth! It may look like a lot of ingredients, but remember that this is a large cake baked in a 12 × 17-inch jellyroll pan.

YIELD: 24 squares

INGREDIENTS

FOR THE CAKE

1 cup granulated sugar

1 cup brown sugar, packed

2 cups all-purpose flour

1 teaspoon salt

1 teaspoon baking soda

2 eggs

½ cup buttermilk

1 teaspoon vanilla

¼ cup Creamy Biscoff Spread

1 cup water

½ cup butter

1 cup chocolate chips, optional

FOR THE FROSTING

½ cup butter

⅓ cup buttermilk

½ cup Creamy Biscoff Spread

3½ cups powdered sugar

1 tablespoon vanilla extract

INSTRUCTIONS

FOR THE CAKE

1. Preheat oven to 375°F. Spray a 12 × 17-inch jellyroll pan with nonstick cooking spray.

2. Whisk together the sugars, flour, salt, and baking soda. Set aside.

3. In a separate bowl whisk together the eggs, buttermilk, and vanilla. Set aside.

4. In a medium saucepan bring Biscoff Spread, water, and butter to a boil. Remove from heat and add the dry ingredients followed by the egg mixture. Stir well and transfer to prepared pan. Sprinkle with chocolate chips if desired.

5. Bake for 15–17 minutes until a toothpick placed in the center comes out clean.

FOR THE FROSTING

6. Bring butter, buttermilk, and Biscoff Spread to a boil. Remove from heat and stir in the powdered sugar followed by the vanilla. The frosting will be thick.

7. Pour evenly over the cake while the cake is still warm from the oven and the frosting is still hot.

Biscoff Truffle Mousse Cheesecake

This cheesecake is a showstopper. It's a fluffy, thick cheesecake baked on a Biscoff cookie crust, topped with a thick layer of creamy Biscoff Truffle Mousse. You may even want to drizzle some *Creamy Biscoff Ice Cream Topping* on top! I originally developed this recipe for our tenth wedding anniversary. Sometimes I can't believe that I get to spend every day with my best friend, but it's true! We laugh every day and enjoy spending time together even after all these years. Believe me when I say I count my blessings! I don't know what he sees in me; maybe he just keeps me around for the cheesecake.

YIELD: 10–12 servings

INGREDIENTS

FOR THE CRUST

2 cups crushed Biscoff cookies (32 cookies)

¼ cup butter, melted

FOR THE CHEESECAKE

1¼ cup granulated sugar

4 (8 oz) sticks of cream cheese, softened

4 eggs

¾ cup heavy cream

1 tablespoon vanilla extract

FOR THE BISCOFF TRUFFLE MOUSSE

8 oz cream cheese, softened

⅔ cup Creamy Biscoff Spread

1 tablespoon milk

2 cups powdered sugar

16 oz nondairy whipped topping (2 small tubs)

INSTRUCTIONS

FOR THE CRUST

1. Preheat oven to 350°F. Wrap the bottom and sides of a 9-inch springform pan in heavy-duty foil. Spray the foil with nonstick cooking spray.

2. Mix together crushed Biscoff cookies and melted butter and press into the bottom of your pan and up the sides. Bake for 7 minutes and cool on a wire rack.

FOR THE CHEESECAKE

1. In a large bowl using a handheld mixer or stand mixer fitted with a paddle attachment, beat the sugar and cream cheese and mix until smooth, about 3 minutes. Add eggs, one at a time, making sure to scrape down the bowl in between each egg. Add heavy cream and vanilla and mix until creamy and smooth.

(CONTINUED ON PAGE 90)

2. Pour batter into prepared crust. Place pan into a larger 10 × 10-inch pan and pour hot water into the larger pan until it reaches halfway up the side of the cheesecake pan. This water bath will keep the cheesecake from drying out and cracking while baking.

3. Bake 50–55 minutes until the edges appear to be set. The center will still have a little bit of a jiggle to it. Close the oven door, turn the heat off, and let rest in the cooling oven for 1 hour.

4. After 1 hour has passed, remove the cheesecake from the water bath and place on a cooling rack to cool completely. Once the cake is completely cooled, chill for at least 5 hours or overnight.

FOR THE BISCOFF TRUFFLE MOUSSE

1. In a large bowl using a handheld mixer or stand mixer fitted with a paddle attachment, combine the cream cheese, Biscoff Spread, and milk until smooth, about 2 minutes.

2. Add powdered sugar ½ cup at a time until fully incorporated. Fold in nondairy whipped topping.

3. Spoon mousse over the cheesecake and level off. Reserve about 1 cup of mousse if you would like to pipe a decorative edge around the top.

4. Chill at least 2 more hours until the mousse is set. Release from the springform pan, slice, and serve.

Chocolate Espresso Biscoff Cupcakes

Save room for dessert! These cupcakes are a chocolate Biscoff lover's dream—moist espresso cupcakes filled with Biscoff Spread, topped with chocolate, Biscoff cookie crumbles, and *Biscoff Buttercream*, then drizzled with *Biscoff Glaze*.

YIELD: 24 cupcakes

INGREDIENTS

1½ cups all-purpose flour

⅔ cup unsweetened cocoa powder

1½ teaspoons baking powder

1 teaspoon baking soda

½ teaspoon salt

1 tablespoon instant coffee granules or espresso powder

10 tablespoons unsalted butter, softened

1½ cups granulated sugar

1 cup buttermilk

3 eggs

2 teaspoons vanilla extract

½ cup Creamy Biscoff Spread

1 cup chocolate chips, melted

8 Biscoff cookies, crumbled

Biscoff Buttercream (page 144)

Biscoff Glaze (page 150)

INSTRUCTIONS

1. Preheat oven to 350°F. Line a muffin tin with 24 paper liners or coat generously with nonstick cooking spray.

2. Whisk together flour, cocoa powder, baking powder, baking soda, salt, and coffee granules in a medium bowl. Set aside.

3. In a large bowl using a handheld mixer or stand mixer fitted with a paddle attachment, cream the butter and sugar until fluffy and lighter in color. Slowly add buttermilk, eggs, and vanilla. Add the dry ingredients ½ cup at a time to the wet ingredients in your mixer bowl until incorporated, about 2 minutes.

4. Spoon batter into prepared tin, filling ¾ full. Bake for 15–18 minutes until a toothpick inserted into a cupcake comes out clean. Cool cupcakes on a wire rack.

5. Use a small paring knife to hollow out the center of each cupcake and fill with 1 teaspoon Biscoff Spread. Replace cake tops if desired. Dip the cupcakes in melted chocolate and sprinkle with Biscoff cookie crumbs. When chocolate is set, pipe with *Biscoff Buttercream* and drizzle with *Biscoff Glaze*.

BREAD & MUFFINS

Biscoff Apple Pie Muffins

Perfect for fall baking, these apple pie muffins make your kitchen smell amazing. They disappear quickly, too. You might not be able to resist grabbing one every time you walk past them! To shred cored apples, place them in a food processor or powerful blender and pulse. No need to drain juices before adding to the batter.

YIELD: 18 muffins

INGREDIENTS

2 cups all-purpose flour

1 cup brown sugar, packed

2 teaspoons baking powder

1 teaspoon ground cinnamon

½ teaspoon nutmeg

½ teaspoon salt

2 medium apples, shredded (approximately 1½ cups)

1 cup Greek yogurt

½ cup Creamy Biscoff Spread

¼ cup vegetable or canola oil

1 egg

1 teaspoon vanilla extract

Cinnamon sugar (1 teaspoon ground cinnamon + 3 tablespoons granulated sugar), optional

INSTRUCTIONS

1. Line a muffin tin with paper liners. Set aside. Preheat oven to 400°F.

2. In a medium bowl whisk together flour, brown sugar, baking powder, cinnamon, nutmeg, and salt. Set aside.

3. In a large bowl using a handheld mixer or stand mixer fitted with a paddle attachment, mix apples, yogurt, Biscoff Spread, oil, egg, and vanilla.

4. Slowly add dry ingredients to the wet and mix until just combined.

5. Spoon batter into paper liners and bake for 18–20 minutes until a toothpick placed in the center comes out clean. Sprinkle with cinnamon sugar while still warm if desired. Let cool completely.

Apple pie spice may be substituted for the other spices. If using, omit cinnamon and nutmeg and replace with 2 teaspoons apple pie spice.

Biscoff Banana Streusel Muffins

I refer to these as "Coffee Shop Muffins" because they are something that I would pay money for at a coffee shop. The streusel topping is so pretty and flavorful sitting on top of the soft, tender muffin. They're perfect for breakfast, brunch, or an afternoon snack.

YIELD: 18 muffins

INGREDIENTS

FOR THE TOPPING

5 tablespoons butter

⅔ cup flour

⅔ cup powdered sugar

¼ teaspoon cinnamon

Pinch of salt (optional)

FOR THE MUFFINS

2 cups all-purpose flour

1 teaspoon baking soda

½ teaspoon baking powder

¼ teaspoon salt

3 ripe bananas

½ cup butter, softened

½ cup Creamy Biscoff Spread

¾ cup brown sugar, packed

2 eggs, beaten

INSTRUCTIONS

1. Prepare the topping: Melt butter in the bottom of a medium microwave-safe bowl. Add flour, powdered sugar, cinnamon, and salt. Stir with a fork until clumps form. Set aside in the refrigerator while preparing the muffins.

2. Preheat oven to 350°F. Line a muffin tin with paper liners or spray with nonstick cooking spray.

3. Whisk together flour, baking soda, baking powder, and salt. Set aside.

4. In a large bowl using a handheld mixer or stand mixer fitted with a paddle attachment, whip bananas 3–4 minutes until light and fluffy. Transfer to a separate bowl and set aside.

5. In a large bowl using a handheld mixer or stand mixer fitted with a paddle attachment, cream butter, Biscoff Spread, and brown sugar 2 minutes until light and fluffy. There is no need to wash the mixer bowl from the previous step. Add eggs one at a time, then mix in the banana.

6. Slowly add dry ingredients to the wet and mix until just combined.

Biscoff Cream Scones

I had never loved a scone until I had one made by my friend Jess. I was a bit skeptical at first but she really does make the most perfectly tender cream scones. She brought me scones when I came home from the hospital with both of my babies, and she's quick to bring me a plate when I'm sick. Isn't she pretty amazing? One day we made them together and I've been hooked ever since. These *Biscoff Cream Scones* are my version.

YIELD: 8 scones

INGREDIENTS

2 cups all-purpose flour

1 tablespoon baking powder

¼ cup brown sugar, packed

½ teaspoon salt

5 tablespoons butter, chilled and cubed into 20 pieces

1 cup heavy cream

¼ cup Creamy Biscoff Spread

1 tablespoon raw cane sugar (granulated may be substituted)

INSTRUCTIONS

1. Preheat oven to 400°F. Spray an 8-inch round cake pan with nonstick cooking spray. Set aside.

2. In a medium bowl whisk together flour, baking powder, brown sugar, and salt.

3. Use a pastry blender or two knives to quickly cut in butter until mixture resembles coarse sand with a few larger butter lumps.

4. Add cream and mix until a rough dough ball begins to form. A stand mixer fitted with a paddle attachment may also be used if you only mix for less than 1 minute. As soon as the dough begins to form, remove it from the bowl and shape into 2 balls. Press the first into the bottom of the cake pan. Spread Biscoff over the entire disk. Press second dough ball into a disk and place on top. Cut into 8 pieces and place pieces onto an ungreased cookie sheet lined with parchment paper or a silicone baking mat. Sprinkle with sugar before baking.

5. Bake for 12–15 minutes until golden brown. Serve warm or enjoy at room temperature.

Biscoff Pumpkin Bread

Every Thursday during college I walked through campus to my friend and mentor Beth's home, where we made a new bread every week—yeast bread, quick bread, sweet rolls, dinner rolls, peasant bread, and more. Many years later we're still very close and I can only hope that I'm as good a friend to her as she has been to me. The pumpkin bread brings back the fondest memories: since my boyfriend (now husband) and I were far from home, we shared Thanksgiving with Beth and her family every year. We always enjoyed pumpkin bread with lots of fresh butter.

YIELD: 2 loaves or 24 muffins

INGREDIENTS

3⅓ cups all-purpose flour

2 teaspoons baking soda

½ teaspoon baking powder

½ teaspoon salt

2 teaspoons pumpkin pie spice

1 teaspoon nutmeg

1 teaspoon cinnamon

4 eggs

½ cup Creamy Biscoff Spread

1 (16 oz) can pumpkin purée

2 cups granulated sugar

¾ cup vegetable or canola oil

⅔ cup water

2 teaspoons vanilla extract

2 cups dark-chocolate chips, optional

INSTRUCTIONS

1. Preheat oven to 325°F. Spray 2 loaf pans with nonstick cooking spray.

2. In a medium bowl whisk together flour, baking soda, baking powder, salt, pumpkin pie spice, nutmeg, and cinnamon. Set aside.

3. In a large bowl using a handheld mixer or stand mixer fitted with a paddle attachment, mix eggs, Biscoff Spread, pumpkin, sugar, oil, water, and vanilla on low speed for 1 minute. Slowly add the dry ingredients ½ cup at a time. Stir in chocolate chips if using.

4. Divide batter evenly into the prepared pans. Bake 1 hour until a toothpick inserted in the center comes out clean.

The best thing about this recipe is that it can be made into muffins as well. My husband's extended family has come to expect these muffins studded with dark-chocolate chips each Thanksgiving meal. These muffins are the very first thing that go into my oven early Thanksgiving morning and the last thing that everyone is nibbling on at the end of the day. Bake muffins at 350°F for 12–15 minutes.

Biscoff Swirl Muffins

These muffins are perfect to serve at breakfast or brunch alongside some fresh fruit. The Biscoff swirl makes for a pretty presentation as well as adding a rich flavor to the muffins. They come together quickly using simple pantry ingredients that you probably already have at home.

YIELD: 12 muffins

INGREDIENTS

1¾ cups all-purpose flour

2 teaspoons baking powder

¼ teaspoon salt

¾ cup butter, softened

¾ cup granulated sugar

3 eggs

1 tablespoon vanilla extract

¾ cup Creamy Biscoff Spread

INSTRUCTIONS

1. Preheat oven to 325°F. Line a muffin tin with paper liners or spray with nonstick cooking spray.

2. In a medium bowl whisk together flour, baking powder, and salt. Set aside.

3. In a large bowl using a handheld mixer or stand mixer fitted with a paddle attachment, cream together butter and sugar for 2 minutes until light and fluffy. Add eggs one at a time, followed by vanilla.

4. Slowly add dry ingredients to the wet and mix until just combined.

5. Spoon batter into paper liners.

6. Melt Biscoff Spread in the microwave for 15–30 seconds. Drop about 1 tablespoon of Biscoff Spread on top of each muffin and use a toothpick to swirl around.

7. Bake for 15–18 minutes until a toothpick placed in the center comes out clean. Cool on a wire rack.

Biscoff Banana Bread

I am so very blessed to have made it through my school years with five best friends. We grew up together and stayed close to one another throughout boyfriends, teenage drama, college life across different parts of the country, marriage, babies, sickness, moves, and more. When I eat banana bread I think of Laurie, Connie, Kami, Sarah, and Meg. We've enjoyed countless conversations around a loaf of banana bread and a pot of coffee. I am grateful for friendship . . . and good banana bread!

YIELD: 2 loaves

INGREDIENTS

2 cups all-purpose flour

1 teaspoon baking soda

½ teaspoon baking powder

½ teaspoon ground cinnamon

¼ teaspoon salt

4 ripe bananas

½ cup butter, softened

½ cup Creamy Biscoff Spread

¾ cup brown sugar, packed

2 eggs

INSTRUCTIONS

1. Preheat oven to 325°F. Spray two 9 × 5-inch loaf pans with nonstick cooking spray. Set aside.

2. In a medium bowl whisk together flour, baking soda, baking powder, cinnamon, and salt. Set aside.

3. In a large bowl using a handheld mixer or stand mixer fitted with a paddle attachment, whip bananas 3–4 minutes until light and fluffy. Transfer to a separate bowl and set aside.

4. In a large bowl using a handheld mixer or stand mixer fitted with a paddle attachment, cream butter, Biscoff Spread, and brown sugar 2 minutes until light and fluffy. There is no need to wash the mixer bowl from the previous step. Add eggs one at a time, then mix in the bananas.

5. Slowly add dry ingredients to the wet and mix until just combined. Do not overmix!

6. Pour batter into prepared loaf pans. Bake for 45–50 minutes until a toothpick placed in the center comes out clean.

Cinnamon-Sugar Biscoff Soft Pretzel Nuggets

If you think you can't make homemade soft pretzels you're wrong! Once you realize how easy these are you will be craving pretzels every day. If you are intimidated by the process of stuffing the pretzels at first, you can adjust the recipe and just heat up a big bowl of Biscoff for dipping. But promise me that you'll try the stuffed version too—they're messy but oh so worth it!

YIELD: Varies depending on size

INGREDIENTS

1 package active dry yeast (2¼ teaspoons)

2 tablespoons brown sugar, packed

1½ cups warm water (110–115°F.)

1 teaspoon salt

4 cups all-purpose flour

1 cup Creamy Biscoff Spread

¼ cup baking soda

4 cups water

3 tablespoons butter, melted

½ cup granulated sugar

½ teaspoon ground cinnamon

INSTRUCTIONS

1. In the bowl of your mixer (fitted with dough hook) dissolve yeast and brown sugar in warm water. Let bloom for about 5 minutes. Add salt and flour to the bowl. Mix with dough hook until a soft, smooth, elastic dough forms, about 8 minutes. The dough should pull away from the sides of the mixer.

2. Transfer to a large glass bowl that has been sprayed with cooking spray. Cover with plastic wrap and place in a warm spot free from drafts. Let rise until doubled, about 1 hour.

3. Place 1 cup Creamy Biscoff Spread in a cake-decorating piping bag or large resealable plastic bag with the tip cut off. Set aside.

4. Turn dough out to a lightly floured surface. Divide the dough into 8 equal pieces. Roll a piece into a rope about 15 inches long. Using your thumb, make a well down the length of the rope.

(CONTINUED ON PAGE 111)

Pipe with Biscoff Spread. Gather the dough around the Biscoff and pinch the seams to seal. Cut into 1-inch pieces to make pretzel bites. Continue to pinch together the seams. Place on floured plate or tray. Set aside and continue for each rope.

5. In a large pot add the baking soda to 4 cups of water and bring to a boil.

6. Working in batches (about 10 nuggets at a time), boil the pretzel nuggets for 30 seconds.

Using a slotted spoon remove to an ungreased cookie sheet that has been lined with parchment paper or a silicone baking mat. Make sure the nuggets are not touching. When baking sheet is full, bake for 15–18 minutes. Repeat with remaining nuggets.

7. When finished baking, brush with melted butter and roll in cinnamon sugar. Pretzels are best enjoyed warm.

Sweet Biscoff Loaf

When I was in college, I enjoyed baking a sweet peanut-butter bread loaf—simply irresistible when topped with strawberry jam. I made that bread every spare chance I got and my friends loved when I would bring it into the dorm to share. It has been years since I've pulled out that well-loved handwritten recipe card. I hope you enjoy this Biscoff version—it's a sweet and dense quick bread that is also perfect slathered with butter or jam.

YIELD: 1 loaf

INGREDIENTS

1½ cups all-purpose flour

1 tablespoon baking powder

1 teaspoon salt

1 cup Creamy Biscoff Spread

⅔ cup granulated sugar

2 eggs

1 teaspoon vanilla extract

1 cup milk

INSTRUCTIONS

1. Preheat oven to 325°F. Spray a 9 × 5-inch loaf pan with nonstick cooking spray. Set aside.

2. In a medium bowl whisk together flour, baking powder, and salt. Set aside.

3. In a large bowl using a handheld mixer or stand mixer fitted with a paddle attachment, cream together Biscoff Spread and sugar for 2 minutes until light and fluffy. Add eggs one at a time followed by vanilla and milk.

4. Slowly add dry ingredients to the wet and mix until just combined.

5. Pour batter into prepared loaf pan. Bake for 50 minutes until a toothpick placed in the center comes out clean. Let cool in the pan for 15 minutes before transferring to a wire rack to cool completely.

Double Chocolate Biscoff Bread

This bread can be enjoyed at breakfast or brunch and as a snack or dessert. The beautiful swirls make it the perfect loaf for entertaining.

YIELD: 1 loaf

INGREDIENTS

1½ cups all-purpose flour

1 tablespoon baking powder

1 teaspoon salt

1 cup Creamy Biscoff Spread

⅔ cup granulated sugar

2 eggs

1 teaspoon vanilla extract

1 cup milk

1 tablespoon cocoa powder

1 cup dark-chocolate chips

INSTRUCTIONS

1. Preheat oven to 325°F. Spray a 9 x 5-inch loaf pan with nonstick cooking spray. Set aside.

2. In a medium bowl whisk together flour, baking powder, and salt. Set aside.

3. In a large bowl using a handheld mixer or stand mixer fitted with a paddle attachment, cream together Biscoff Spread and sugar for 2 minutes until light and fluffy. Add eggs one at a time followed by vanilla and milk.

4. Slowly add dry ingredients to the wet and mix until just combined.

5. Remove 1 cup of batter and add the cocoa powder to it. Stir in chocolate chips.

6. Pour batter into prepared loaf pan, alternating between the 2 kinds. Run a butter knife through the pan once in a figure-8 pattern. Top with a few more chocolate chips if desired.

7. Bake for 50 minutes until a toothpick placed in the center comes out clean. Let cool in the pan for 15 minutes before transferring to a wire rack to cool completely.

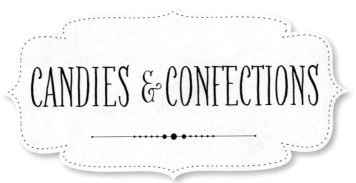

CANDIES & CONFECTIONS

Biscoff Marshmallow Fudge Bars

These bars are a quick fudge that takes a shortcut from a can of store-bought frosting. I call it Cheater Fudge. The marshmallow centers are a fun surprise too!

YIELD: 36 Bars

INGREDIENTS

2 cups chocolate chips

½ cup Creamy Biscoff Spread

1 (16 oz) can store-bought chocolate frosting

2 cups mini marshmallows

INSTRUCTIONS

1. Line a 9 x 9-inch baking dish with aluminum foil or parchment paper, leaving at least 1 inch hanging over the sides. Spray with nonstick cooking spray.

2. Heat chocolate chips in a large microwave-safe bowl for 30-second intervals until melted. Immediately stir in Biscoff Spread and frosting. Stir until smooth.

3. Working quickly, pour half of the fudge into the bottom of prepared pan. Sprinkle marshmallows, then top with remaining fudge. Use a spatula that has been sprayed with cooking spray to press the fudge down. Let set up in the refrigerator at least 1 hour before serving.

Biscoff Candy Cups

Make your own candy at home! This recipe is especially perfect for the person who misses out on enjoying the traditional peanut butter version of this classic candy. Everyone will enjoy indulging in one . . . or two . . . or three of these mini candy cups.

YIELD: 3½ dozen candies

INGREDIENTS

½ cup butter, softened

1 cup Creamy or Crunchy Biscoff Spread

1½ cups powdered sugar

3½ cups dark or milk chocolate chips or discs

1 tablespoon shortening, optional

As a shortcut you can purchase prepared chocolate cups and use the dough recipe above, or pipe in Creamy Biscoff Spread. Top with more chocolate and let set.

INSTRUCTIONS

1. In a large bowl using a handheld mixer or stand mixer fitted with a paddle attachment, cream the butter and Biscoff Spread. Slowly add in powdered sugar ½ cup at a time. Mix until incorporated.

2. Roll out dough into approximately 40 balls small enough to fit into the wells of a mini muffin tin. Set each dough ball onto a baking sheet or large plate and let chill in the refrigerator while you prepare your chocolate.

3. Line a mini muffin tin with paper or foil liners.

4. In a microwave-safe bowl melt chocolate for 30–60 seconds. Stir and return to microwave for 30–60 more seconds until melted. Add up to 1 tablespoon shortening to thin out the chocolate and make for easier pouring if necessary.

5. Spoon a thin chocolate base into the bottom of each paper liner. Remove Biscoff dough from the refrigerator. Place 1 dough ball into each well, leaving room on the sides for chocolate. Fill the rest of the liner with chocolate. Return to the refrigerator to set, at least 30 minutes.

Biscoff Cereal Snack Mix

Everybody has a family member who loves this cereal snack mix. You know the recipe I'm talking about. We've been eating it the same way for years but recently many more varieties and recipes have become available. Now you can find every version you could ever imagine and more! Of course I created a Biscoff one for you. Enjoy!

INGREDIENTS

6 cups square rice cereal

1 cup powdered sugar

½ cup Biscoff cookies, crushed

¼ cup butter, softened

1 cup white chocolate chips

½ cup Creamy or Crunchy Biscoff Spread

INSTRUCTIONS

1. Place cereal in a large bowl. Set aside.

2. Place powdered sugar and crushed Biscoff cookies in a large resealable plastic bag. Set aside.

3. On the stovetop over medium-low heat, melt butter, white chocolate chips, and Biscoff Spread together. Stir until smooth.

4. Pour white chocolate mixture over cereal and gently toss until coated. Try to avoid crushing the cereal.

5. Transfer to the resealable plastic bag and shake until coated evenly with powdered-sugar mixture. Remove from bag and let cool in a large bowl or on a baking sheet or tray.

Biscoff Cookie S'mores

My husband has a new love of camping. He will sometimes ride his bike hundreds of miles in one day, carrying all of his camping equipment, clothes, and food on his bicycle so that he can set up a tent and sleep on the ground. Then he packs it all up in the morning and rides home. You could say that I'm just not as adventurous as he is. Camping may not be my favorite, but I can bring the s'mores.

YIELD: 4 servings

INGREDIENTS

Biscoff cookies

Milk chocolate chips, melted

Creamy Biscoff Spread

Toasted marshmallows

INSTRUCTIONS

1. Dip the bottoms of Biscoff cookies into a thin layer of chocolate. Set on parchment paper to cool.

2. Spread Creamy Biscoff Spread on each cookie and sandwich two together with a marshmallow in between.

Alternately you could spread the Creamy Biscoff Spread on top of the cookies and place a piece of chocolate on top, followed by a marshmallow and another cookie. Either way, it's going to taste amazing!

Biscoff Cookie Toffee

This is your warning: homemade toffee is addictive. I've been known to make three batches right in a row. This toffee has found a place on my holiday baking and candy list. Everyone loves it and it is impossible to have just one taste!

YIELD: 36 pieces

INGREDIENTS

20–30 Biscoff cookies

1 cup salted butter

1 cup white sugar

1 teaspoon vanilla extract

1 cup milk chocolate chips

Biscoff cookie crumbles

INSTRUCTIONS

1. Line a 9 x 9-inch baking dish with Biscoff cookies. Set aside.

2. Melt butter in a heavy saucepan over medium heat. Add sugar.

3. Stir constantly for 6–8 minutes until the color is light brown (like a paper bag). If using a candy thermometer the temperature should reach about 298°F. The mixture may look curdled or may separate—that's okay. You are looking for a light brown caramel color.

4. Remove from heat and slowly add vanilla, being careful to avoid any splatters to your skin. Stir for a few more seconds, and pour over the cookies. Immediately sprinkle with chocolate chips. Let the chocolate melt for a few minutes, then spread with a knife. Sprinkle with Biscoff cookie crumbles.

5. Let the toffee cool for at least 1 hour. Use a knife to break into pieces.

Biscoff Crunch Fudge

These little fudge squares are so rich and delicious. One bite and you'll be hooked! They would make a perfect addition to any dessert tray.

YIELD: 36 pieces

INGREDIENTS

½ cup unsalted butter

1 cup granulated sugar

½ cup heavy cream

2½ cups white chocolate chips

7 oz Marshmallow Fluff

20 Biscoff cookies, crushed

¼ cup Creamy Biscoff Spread, melted

INSTRUCTIONS

1. Line a 9 × 9-inch baking dish with aluminum foil or parchment paper, leaving at least 1 inch hanging over the sides. Spray with nonstick cooking spray.

2. In a large saucepan over medium heat combine butter, sugar, and heavy cream. Stir constantly until mixture begins to boil.

3. Remove from heat. Stir in the white chocolate and Marshmallow Fluff until melted and smooth. Fold in crushed Biscoff cookies.

4. Pour fudge into prepared baking dish. Drizzle with melted Biscoff Spread. Allow time for the fudge to set up. Refrigerate at least 3 hours before serving.

Biscoff Tiger Bark

Traditional tiger bark gets a modern makeover! I made this recipe the very first time I swapped peanut butter for Biscoff Spread. It was my "aha" moment in the early days of peanut-free living. This little treat was my first attempt at converting our favorite recipes to make them safe for my son. Be sure to choose a chocolate that is certified nut-free, and you'll have an easy and delicious classic treat that can be enjoyed by everyone.

YIELD: Varies

INGREDIENTS

2 cups white chocolate chips or discs

½ cup Creamy or Crunchy Biscoff Spread

1 cup milk chocolate chips

6-8 Biscoff cookies, coarsely chopped, optional

Because this recipe is so very simple and beautiful, it makes a great classroom treat for school-aged children if your child's school allows homemade birthday treats.

INSTRUCTIONS

1. Line a rimmed baking sheet with foil or parchment paper. Alternatively you can use small silicone molds (no greasing necessary).

2. Heat white chocolate in a microwave-safe bowl for 30-second intervals until melted. Immediately stir in Biscoff Spread and stir until smooth.

3. In a separate bowl heat milk chocolate in a microwave-safe bowl for 30-second intervals until melted.

4. Pour white chocolate/Biscoff mixture into your prepared pan (you may need to reheat it again). Drizzle the milk chocolate on top and swirl around the pan with a butter knife to get a marbled look.

5. Immediately sprinkle with chopped cookies if desired. Let cool. When set, cut into pieces or remove from silicone molds.

Biscoff Buckeye Truffles

Buckeye candies have a very special place in our family. For the past 15 years around the holidays I've sat down with my mother-in-law to make hundreds (sometimes nearing a thousand!) of these candies. Now I have the pleasure of having a sister-in-law, so she joins us as well and the three of us spend the day retelling old stories and catching up with one another. We look forward to it not only because of the memories to be made, but because of the rich tradition it holds for our family. Our recipe dates from 1963, and thanks to Biscoff spread, we're able to swap the traditional peanut butter for Biscoff and serve it at home.

YIELD: 20 pieces

INGREDIENTS

½ cup butter, softened

½ cup Creamy Biscoff Spread

1 teaspoon vanilla extract

2 cups powdered sugar

2 cups milk chocolate chips or disks

1 tablespoon shortening, optional

2 crushed Biscoff cookies, optional

INSTRUCTIONS

1. In a large bowl using a handheld mixer or stand mixer fitted with a paddle attachment, cream butter, Biscoff Spread, and vanilla for 2 minutes until light and fluffy.

2. Slowly add the powdered sugar in ½ cup increments.

3. Roll dough into approximately 20 balls. Set aside.

4. In a microwave-safe bowl, melt chocolate for 30–60 seconds. Stir and return to microwave for 30–60 more seconds until melted. Add up to 1 tablespoon shortening to thin out the chocolate and make for easier dipping if necessary.

5. Using a spoon, dip the truffles into the chocolate. Place on parchment paper to set. Cover truffles completely and sprinkle with crushed Biscoff cookies if desired, or leave the tops exposed to resemble buckeyes. Store in an airtight container.

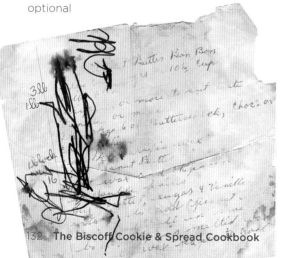

Brown Sugar Biscoff-Crunch Ice Cream

This homemade Biscoff ice cream is impossibly fluffy and delicious. This recipe was inspired by a Biscoff gelato that I had in Orlando sitting with my friends at a food blogging conference. Many people look at me funny when I say that I've made real friends over the Internet. I never imagined that publishing a food blog would foster so many friendships through a community of food bloggers. But it's true! My life is definitely more fun because of these ladies. There are way too many to list—you know who you are!

YIELD: 6-8 servings

INGREDIENTS

1 cup whole milk

¾ cup brown sugar, packed

Pinch of salt

2 cups heavy cream

1 tablespoon vanilla

10 Biscoff cookies, crushed

½ cup Creamy Biscoff Spread, melted

INSTRUCTIONS

1. In the bowl of your mixer whisk together milk, brown sugar, and salt until the sugar is dissolved.

2. Beat in heavy cream and vanilla. Transfer to a lidded bowl and refrigerate 4 hours or overnight. You want this mixture to be really cold before transferring to the ice cream maker.

3. Add chilled mixture to ice cream maker and churn according to directions. Add Biscoff cookies during the final 2 minutes of churning.

4. Once churned, transfer ice cream to a lidded container. As you are scooping the ice cream into the container, drizzle with Biscoff Spread. Cover and freeze 2 hours until firm. Alternately you can enjoy it right away with a soft-serve consistency.

Butterscotch Biscoff Trifle

After having a food allergy diagnosed in your family, there are some recipes that you just miss. Fortunately my son was diagnosed as a toddler so he doesn't really have a taste for peanuts or peanut butter treats. This trifle recipe is based on a classic dessert I had growing up—a very popular butterscotch trifle. The candies that are typically used are not safe for my son, so I came up with this alternative. I should note that my son has always been able to eat boxed pudding mix without incident. Every person is different. As always, be sure to read labels and make informed decisions about the food you eat.

INGREDIENTS

2 large (5.1 oz) packages butterscotch pudding

½ cup Creamy Biscoff Spread

4 cups milk

9 x 13-inch pan of prepared brownies (I used *Fudgy Biscoff Swirl Brownies,* page 52)

32 Biscoff cookies

16 oz nondairy whipped topping

INSTRUCTIONS

1. In a large bowl using a handheld mixer or stand mixer fitted with a paddle attachment, combine pudding mix, Biscoff Spread, and milk. Stir for 2 minutes and let set up in the refrigerator while you prepare the first layer of the trifle.

2. Cut brownies into 24 squares. Set aside 4 squares and chop those up into even smaller squares for garnish on top.

3. Begin layering the trifle dish with brownies, followed by pudding, Biscoff cookies, and whipped topping. Continue layering until you've reached the top of your trifle dish. Garnish with reserved brownie pieces and coarsely chopped Biscoff cookies.

4. Refrigerate until ready to serve. You'll want to serve this within 6 hours of preparing. Any longer than 6 hours, the layers get soggy.

White Chocolate Biscoff Granola Bites

These sweet white chocolate granola bites taste like candy. Even the pickiest eaters won't have a problem eating their oats. My brother asked me to make these again about four times before he was finished eating just one; they're that addicting!

YIELD: 16 bites

INGREDIENTS

1 cup crispy rice cereal

1 cup old-fashioned oats

⅓ cup honey

⅓ cup Creamy or Crunchy Biscoff Spread

⅓ cup white chocolate chips or discs

2 tablespoons butter

3 tablespoons white chocolate, melted, optional for garnish

INSTRUCTIONS

1. Line an 8 × 8-inch baking dish with aluminum foil or parchment paper, leaving at least 1 inch hanging over the sides. Spray with nonstick cooking spray.

2. Place cereal and oats in a medium bowl. Stir and set aside.

3. Heat honey, Biscoff Spread, white chocolate, and butter over low to medium heat on stovetop, stirring constantly until melted and heated through.

4. Pour wet ingredients over the dry ingredients and mix to combine.

5. Transfer into prepared dish and press down using greased hands that have been sprayed with nonstick cooking spray. Let set up for 20 minutes.

6. Lift out of pan and cut into 16 even pieces. Roll into balls, making sure to squeeze firm while rolling. Drizzle with more melted white chocolate if desired. The granola bites will seem sticky as you roll them from the honey squeezed out during rolling. This is okay; the honey is necessary as a binder in the recipe. The granola bites will firm up and set when cooled completely. Store in an airtight container.

FROSTINGS & FILLINGS

Biscoff Breakfast Syrup

This creamy syrup will make any breakfast extraordinary. Try it on *Quick Biscoff Waffles* (page 13) or *Biscoff Cheesecake-Stuffed French Toast* (page 14).

YIELD: 6-8 servings

INGREDIENTS

¼ cup Creamy Biscoff Spread

¼ cup sweetened condensed milk

¼ cup maple syrup

INSTRUCTIONS

1. Melt Biscoff Spread in a microwave-safe bowl for 30 seconds.

2. Add condensed milk and maple syrup. Whisk until smooth.

What to do with the opened can of sweetened condensed milk? It's the perfect sweetener for iced coffee!

Biscoff Buttercream

One of the first things I perfected in my kitchen was homemade buttercream frosting. Now I almost never buy canned frosting since our family loves the taste of homemade. I love the versatility. Homemade buttercream is more of a method than a recipe. If you need it thicker for piping, use more powdered sugar, or add more milk if you prefer a thinner consistency. I do suggest heavy cream for homemade frosting.

This Biscoff Buttercream is the perfect addition to any cake or cupcake. I always make more than I need because everyone who walks by as I'm frosting the cake seems to take a spoon to the bowl; it's addicting! Don't say I didn't warn you!

YIELD: 4 cups

INGREDIENTS

1 cup butter, softened

¼ cup Creamy Biscoff Spread

1 tablespoon vanilla extract

4 cups powdered sugar, divided

¼ cup heavy cream (or milk)

This recipe can easily be halved. As written it is enough to frost a two-layer cake, or 24 cupcakes.

If you prefer a crusting buttercream (one that sets firm to the touch) add ½ cup shortening when creaming the butter and Biscoff Spread. You may add more milk or cream if desired.

INSTRUCTIONS

1. In a large bowl using a handheld mixer or stand mixer fitted with a paddle attachment, cream butter and Biscoff Spread until smooth and fluffy, about 4 minutes. Add vanilla.

2. Slowly add 2 cups of powdered sugar.

3. Pour in heavy cream or milk.

4. Gradually incorporate the final 2 cups of the powdered sugar.

5. Mix on low speed until all ingredients are smooth and mixed well. Adjust the consistency by adding more cream or milk if you want a thinner frosting.

Chocolate Biscoff Buttercream

I'm not a huge fan of chocolate frosting. I can't believe I just admitted that! When given the option I will almost always choose vanilla cake and frosting over chocolate. However, this *Chocolate Biscoff Buttercream* is my favorite way to enjoy chocolate frosting. It is silky smooth and perfect for finishing off your favorite cake or brownies.

YIELD: 4 cups

INGREDIENTS

1 cup butter, softened

¼ cup Creamy Biscoff Spread

4 cups powdered sugar, divided

2 tablespoons cocoa powder

¼ cup heavy cream (or milk)

This recipe can easily be halved. As written it is enough to frost a two-layer cake, or 24 cupcakes.

Add up to 1 teaspoon of vanilla if you prefer the taste.

If you prefer a crusting buttercream (one that sets firm to the touch) add ½ cup shortening when creaming the butter and Biscoff Spread. You may add more milk or cream if desired.

INSTRUCTIONS

1. In a large bowl using a handheld mixer or stand mixer fitted with a paddle attachment, cream butter and Biscoff Spread until smooth and fluffy, about 4 minutes.

2. Slowly add 2 cups of powdered sugar and cocoa powder.

3. Pour in heavy cream or milk.

4. Gradually incorporate the final 2 cups of the powdered sugar.

5. Mix on low speed until all ingredients are smooth and mixed well. Adjust the consistency by adding more cream or milk if you want a thinner frosting.

Biscoff Cookie Dough Dip

When developing this recipe, I had to make it three times in the same week! Each time my family gobbled it up before I could grab a quick picture. This dip is a complete dream. Serve it with pretzel sticks or graham crackers . . . but you may find yourself stealing it by the spoonful!

YIELD: 2 cups

INGREDIENTS

½ cup butter, softened

½ cup Creamy Biscoff Spread

¾ cup brown sugar, packed

½ cup all-purpose flour

1 teaspoon vanilla extract

¼ teaspoon salt

¼ cup milk or cream

½ cup mini semisweet chocolate chips

INSTRUCTIONS

1. In a large bowl using a handheld mixer or stand mixer fitted with a paddle attachment, cream the butter, Biscoff Spread, and brown sugar for 2 minutes until light and fluffy.

2. Add the flour, vanilla, and salt. Slowly beat in milk and thin to desired consistency.

3. Fold in the chocolate chips. Chill for at least 30 minutes. Sprinkle with more chocolate chips when ready to serve if desired.

Biscoff Glaze

This easy *Biscoff Glaze* is a simple way to decorate cupcakes and cookies. It will firm up just enough to set. Try it drizzled over *Chocolate Espresso Biscoff Cupcakes* (page 92) or on *Biscoff Cut-Out Cookies* (page 36).

Yield: approximately ¼ cup

INGREDIENTS

¼ cup Creamy Biscoff Spread

3 tablespoons powdered sugar

3 tablespoons milk or cream

INSTRUCTIONS

1. Add all ingredients in a small bowl. Mix until combined.

2. Dip cupcakes, cookies, donuts, and more!

Biscoff Magic Crunch Ice Cream Topping

Okay, so it's more science than magic, but it is pretty magical to watch your ice cream topping go from a liquid to a solid right before your eyes. Most virgin coconut oil becomes a liquid at 75°F. Anything colder than that makes it solidify.

YIELD: approximately ⅓ cup

INGREDIENTS

⅓ cup Creamy or Crunchy Biscoff Spread

1–2 tablespoons virgin coconut oil, melted

2 tablespoons crushed Biscoff cookies

INSTRUCTIONS

1. Stir the ingredients together in a small bowl.

2. Pour over ice cream.

Feel free to omit the cookies and make this a smooth ice cream topping. It will still harden into a shell when it touches the ice cream.

Biscoff Mousse

Creamy no-bake *Biscoff Mousse* piped into mini graham-cracker crusts—decadent and simple at the same time. Our family and friends love this easy dessert. I love it because it can be prepared in advance and pulled out of the refrigerator when ready to serve.

YIELD: 6 servings

INGREDIENTS

4 oz cream cheese

½ cup Creamy Biscoff Spread

1 tablespoon milk or cream

1 cup powdered sugar

8 oz nondairy whipped topping

6 mini graham-cracker piecrusts, optional

Biscoff cookies, crushed, optional

INSTRUCTIONS

1. In a large bowl using a handheld mixer or stand mixer fitted with a paddle attachment, combine the cream cheese, Biscoff Spread, and milk until smooth, about 2 minutes.

2. Add powdered sugar ½ cup at a time until fully incorporated. Fold in nondairy whipped topping.

3. Spoon mousse into 6 small serving containers or mini piecrusts.

4. Chill at least 2 more hours until the mousse is set. Sprinkle with crushed Biscoff cookies if desired.

Biscoff Cream Cheese Frosting

Perfectly creamy and rich, this cream cheese frosting gets a little help from Creamy Biscoff Spread. It is the perfect frosting to accompany the *Biscoff Carrot Cake* (page 73). Due to the cream cheese be sure to refrigerate any treats that use this frosting.

YIELD: 4 cups

INGREDIENTS

8 oz cream cheese, softened

½ cup Creamy Biscoff Spread

1 teaspoon vanilla extract

3 cups powdered sugar, divided

3 tablespoons heavy cream or milk

INSTRUCTIONS

1. In a large bowl using a handheld mixer or stand mixer fitted with a paddle attachment, mix together cream cheese, Biscoff Spread, and vanilla 2 minutes until smooth.

2. Add powdered sugar ½ cup at a time, mixing well between each addition. After about 2 cups, add the cream, then finish off with powdered sugar. Add more cream or milk to desired consistency.

Creamy Biscoff Fruit Dip

Our family's favorite way to enjoy this dip is with apple slices. Be creative and try dipping your favorite fruit. You can bump up the protein by substituting vanilla or plain Greek yogurt in this creamy dip. If Greek yogurt is not sweet enough for you, add 2 tablespoons brown sugar.

YIELD: 1½ cups

INGREDIENTS

½ cup Creamy Biscoff Spread

8 oz cream cheese, softened

½ cup plain or vanilla yogurt

½ teaspoon ground cinnamon

⅛ cup honey

Biscoff cookie crumbles, optional

INSTRUCTIONS

1. In a large bowl using a handheld mixer or stand mixer fitted with a paddle attachment, cream Biscoff Spread and softened cream cheese on medium speed until fluffy.

2. Add yogurt, ground cinnamon, and honey. Beat on low speed until ingredients are fully incorporated.

3. Refrigerate and keep covered until ready to serve.

4. Top with crushed Biscoff cookies if desired. Serve with apple slices, strawberries, pretzels, or Biscoff cookies.

Creamy Biscoff Ice Cream Topping

Cold ice cream with warm, silky-smooth Biscoff topping is the perfect summer treat! My oldest son, Luke, was a trooper while posing for this picture. Little boys aren't exactly known for being still. I had taken only one or two shots to adjust the settings on my camera when I looked up and he had already helped himself to the cherry on top! Well, who can blame him for digging in? As soon as I stepped away, my youngest son Tim got to work with his spoon too!

YIELD: 1½ cups

INGREDIENTS

14 oz sweetened condensed milk

¼ cup butter

½ cup Creamy Biscoff Spread

½ teaspoon vanilla extract

INSTRUCTIONS

Combine all ingredients over medium heat until butter and Biscoff Spread are melted and incorporated. Spoon over ice cream.

ACKNOWLEDGMENTS

To my husband, Chuck—You are my best friend and biggest supporter. I love that we laugh together every day and that we truly enjoy our time spent with one another. You are an amazing husband and father. Our boys are blessed to have such a loving and attentive dad. Thank you for encouraging me to challenge myself and to believe in the gifts and abilities that God has given me. This book could not have happened without your constant love and encouragement.

To Luke—You make me smile every day, and I'm so very happy to be your mom. Thank you for being excited with me as we wrote this book together and for hanging in there even when you just wanted *plain* chocolate chip cookies. Your dad and I love all of your creative ideas and your imagination. We are so very proud of you.

To Timothy—I love every moment with you, and I'm happy to be your mom. Your joy for life makes every day an adventure. Thank you for helping me test all of these recipes for the book and for your enthusiasm as we made many, many Biscoff desserts every day. Your dad and I are so proud to be your parents. We love how caring and compassionate you are.

To my parents, Kip and Maritta—"Thank you" seems so inadequate for the years you put into making me the woman I am today. Thanks for instilling in me a love of baking for others. You always encouraged me to make messes and try new things.

To Grandma Horvath and Grandma Sam—I miss you both so very much. I enjoyed every minute in your kitchens as I learned the art of feeding my family with a smile on my face and joy in my heart.

To Patty—God gave me the perfect mother-in-law in you. Thank you for including me in your traditions and for welcoming me into your family.

To my friends Laurie, Connie, Kami, Sarah, and Megan—I would have never started sharing my recipes online if it had not have been for your prompting and encouragement. Not many people are as blessed as we are to have made it through childhood with five best friends. Oh the fun times we have had through the years, baking thousands of cookies together!

To Ann—Thank you for finding me and for asking me to write this cookbook. I never intended to write a book but you saw an author in me. I appreciate your expertise and guidance.

To Idil, Steffany, and the whole Lotus Bakery team—Thank you for making a product that my family loves. I can't wait to see what's in store for Biscoff!

To my blogging peers and friends, you inspire me every day—Christi Johnstone, Erin Sellin, Amanda Rettke, Karly Campbell, Bridget Edwards, Rachel Currier, Amanda Livesay, Meaghan Mountford, Kristen Doyle, Kita Roberts, and so many more.

To Averie, Amanda, Rachel, Lori, Christi, Bridget, Kristen, and Amanda—Thank you for your support.

To Chuck, Luke, Laura, Rachel, Erin, Colt, Chris, Jessie, Chad, and Megan—Thank you for testing my recipes, for baking them alongside me, and for helping me edit the stories and instructions that go along with them.

To my readers of InKatrinasKitchen.com—we have been on this journey together and I look forward to your comments every day. Your kind, encouraging words make me smile. I have the best job in the world and you are a part of what makes it so fun. Thank you!

INDEX

E

Easy Biscoff Granola, 2, *3*
   Biscoff Yogurt Parfaits, *4, 5*

F

Fillings. *See* Frostings & Fillings
French toast, Biscoff Cheesecake-
   Stuffed, 14, *15*
Frostings & Fillings, 141–161
   Biscoff Breakfast Syrup, *142,*
     143
   Biscoff Buttercream, 144, *145*
   Biscoff Cookie Dough Dip, 148,
     149
   Biscoff Cream Cheese Frosting,
     156, 157
   Biscoff Glaze, 150, *151*
   Biscoff Magic Crunch Ice Cream
     Topping, *152,* 153
   Biscoff Mousse, 154, *155*
   Chocolate Biscoff Buttercream,
     146, 147
   Creamy Biscoff Fruit Dip, 158,
     159
   Creamy Biscoff Ice Cream Top-
     ping, *160,* 161
   Fudgy Biscoff Swirl Brownies, 52,
     53
   Butterscotch Biscoff Trifle, 136,
     137

G

Gooey Caramel Biscoff Brownies,
   54, 55
Graham-cracker piecrusts
   Biscoff Mousse, 154, *155*
Granola, 2
   Easy Biscoff Granola, 2, *3*

Greek yogurt. *See also* Yogurt
   Biscoff Apple Pie Muffins, *96,* 97
   Biscoff Carrot Cake, *72,* 73
   Biscoff Coffee Cakes with Biscoff
     Crumb Topping, 77, *78,* 79

H

Honey-Oat Biscoff Bars, *62,* 63

I

Ice Cream, Brown Sugar Biscoff-
   Crunch, *134,* 135
Ice cream topping
   Creamy Biscoff Ice Cream Top-
     ping, *160,* 161
   Gooey Caramel Biscoff Brown-
     ies, *54,* 55

L

Lotus Bakeries, viii

M

Marshmallow Fluff
   Biscoff Crunch Fudge, 128, *129*
   Biscoff Marshmallow Cereal
     Treat Bars, 64, *65*
Marshmallows
   Biscoff Cookie S'mores, 124, *125*
   Biscoff Marshmallow Cereal
     Treat Bars, 64, *65*
   Biscoff Marshmallow Fudge
     Bars, *118,* 119
Mousse, Biscoff, 154, *155*
Muffins. *See* Breads & Muffins

N

No-Bake Biscoff Bars, 56, *57*

O

Oats
   Biscoff Applesauce Cake, 70, *71*
   Biscoff No-Bake Cookies, *38,* 39
   Biscoff Oatmeal Raisin Cookies,
     40, 41
   Biscoff Overnight Oats, *8,* 9
   Easy Biscoff Granola, 2, *3*
   Honey-Oat Biscoff Bars, *62,* 63
   White Chocolate Biscoff Granola
     Bites, *138,* 139

P

Pancakes, Buttermilk Biscoff, 10,
   11
Parfaits, Biscoff Yogurt, *4, 5*
Pumpkin, Biscoff, Bread, 102, *103*

Q

Quick Biscoff Waffles, *12,* 13

R

Raisins, Biscoff Oatmeal, Cookies,
   40, *41*
Rice cereal. *See* Crispy rice cereal;
   Square rice cereal

S

St. Nicholas's Feast, viii
Scheppers, Els, viii
Scones, Biscoff Cream, *100,* 101
Speculoos, viii
Square rice cereal
   Biscoff Cereal Snack Mix, *122,*
     123
Sweet Biscoff Loaf, *112,* 113
Syrup, Biscoff Breakfast, *142,* 143

ABOUT THE AUTHOR

Katrina Bahl has built a loyal following on her site, InKatrinasKitchen.com, and an active social media community on Facebook, Pinterest, and Instagram. The award-winning site features Bahl's original recipes and photography. Bahl discovered Biscoff spread when her son was diagnosed with a peanut allergy, and she has transferred her love of peanut butter to the cookie butter. Bahl lives in Ohio with her husband and two young sons.

CARRIE NELSON THOMAS / BRENDON THOMAS PHOTOGRAPHY